I0427663

PREFACE

1. Scope

This publication provides joint doctrine for planning and conducting civil-military operations (CMO) by joint forces, employing civil affairs forces, conducting civil affairs operations, and coordinating with departments, agencies, or other organizations during the execution of CMO.

2. Purpose

This publication has been prepared under the direction of the Chairman of the Joint Chiefs of Staff (CJCS). It sets forth joint doctrine to govern the activities and performance of the Armed Forces of the United States in joint operations and provides the doctrinal basis for US military coordination with other US Government departments and agencies during operations and for US military involvement in multinational operations. It provides military guidance for the exercise of authority by combatant commanders and other joint force commanders (JFCs) and prescribes joint doctrine for operations, education, and training. It provides military guidance for use by the Armed Forces in preparing their appropriate plans. It is not the intent of this publication to restrict the authority of the JFC from organizing the force and executing the mission in a manner the JFC deems most appropriate to ensure unity of effort in the accomplishment of the overall objective.

3. Application

a. Joint doctrine established in this publication applies to the Joint Staff, commanders of combatant commands, subordinate unified commands, joint task forces, subordinate components of these commands, the Services, and combat support agencies.

b. The guidance in this publication is authoritative; as such, this doctrine will be followed except when, in the judgment of the commander, exceptional circumstances dictate otherwise. If conflicts arise between the contents of this publication and the contents of Service publications, this publication will take precedence unless the CJCS, normally in coordination with the other members of the Joint Chiefs of Staff, has provided more current and specific guidance. Commanders of forces operating as part of a multinational (alliance or coalition) military command should follow multinational doctrine and procedures ratified by the United States. For doctrine and procedures not ratified by the United States, commanders should evaluate and follow the multinational command's doctrine and procedures, where applicable and consistent with US law, regulations, and doctrine.

For the Chairman of the Joint Chiefs of Staff:

DAVID L. GOLDFEIN, Lt Gen, USAF
Director, Joint Staff

i

Intentionally Blank

SUMMARY OF CHANGES
REVISION OF JOINT PUBLICATION 3-57, DATED 08 JULY 2008

- **Adds new chapter on civil affairs forces and civil affairs operations.**

- **Adds new appendix on civil information management.**

- **Introduces the methodology and organization of "civil-military teams."**

- **Updates roles and responsibilities of Department of Defense and its organizations regarding civil-military operations.**

- **Changes the term "PSYOP" to "MISO" where appropriate.**

- **Updates Appendix A, "Service Capabilities," to comply with current capabilities.**

- **Adds definitions for the terms "civic action, civil information, civil information management, civil-military teams, and military government."**

- **Updates definitions for "civil affairs, civil-military operations, civil-military operations center, indigenous populations and institutions, military civic action, provincial reconstruction team, and private sector."**

- **Removes the term "expellee."**

Intentionally Blank

TABLE OF CONTENTS

Intentionally Blank

EXECUTIVE SUMMARY
COMMANDER'S OVERVIEW

- **Provides an introduction to civil-military operations (CMO).**

- **Describes organization and command relationships for CMO.**

- **Explains CMO planning.**

- **Addresses civil affairs forces and civil affairs operations.**

- **Covers coordination of CMO.**

Introduction to Civil-Military Operations

Civil-Military Operations (CMO)

Civil-military operations (CMO) are the activities of a commander performed by designated civil affairs or other military forces that establish, maintain, influence, or exploit relationships between military forces and indigenous populations and institutions (IPI), by directly supporting the attainment of objectives relating to the reestablishment or maintenance of stability within a region or host nation (HN). At the strategic, operational, and tactical levels of war, and during all military operations, CMO are essential to the military instrument to coordinate the integration of military and nonmilitary instruments of national power, particularly in support of stability, counterinsurgency, and other operations dealing with asymmetric and irregular threats.

CMO and Levels of War

CMO are applicable at the strategic, operational, and tactical levels of war. At the strategic level, CMO focus on larger and long-term issues that may be part of a Department of Defense (DOD) global campaign, or United States Government (USG) reconstruction, economic development initiatives, and stability operations in failing or recovering nations. At the operational level, CMO integrate and synchronize interagency, intergovernmental organization (IGO), and nongovernmental organization (NGO) activities with joint force operations. Often, a civil-military team or civil-military operations center (CMOC) may facilitate tactical-level CMO among the military, the local populace, NGOs, and IGOs.

Components of CMO	CMO include a range of activities that integrate civil and military actions for support to civil administration, populace and resources control, foreign humanitarian assistance, nation assistance, and civil information management. These activities are particularly suited to support the development of a country's material and human resources, or to assist the HN in achieving other national objectives.
CMO, Civil Affairs (CA), and Unified Action	In carrying out their CMO responsibilities, commanders use civil affairs operations (CAO). The relationship between CMO and CAO is best considered within the broad context of unified action that involves the synchronization, coordination, or integration of the activities of governmental and nongovernmental entities with military operations to achieve unity of effort.

Organization and Command Relationships for Civil-Military Operations

Assistant Secretary of Defense for Special Operations and Low-Intensity Conflict	The Assistant Secretary of Defense for Special Operations and Low-Intensity Conflict acts as Office of the Secretary of Defense point of contact for DOD and coordinates CAO as they relate to the activities of interagency partners, IGOs, NGOs, IPI, other organizations, and the private sector, in accordance with applicable laws and regulations to plan and conduct CMO.
Geographic Combatant Commanders	The geographic combatant commanders (GCCs) provide regional coordination and direction to their subordinate commanders for the integration of CMO and CAO into military plans and operations and coordinates CMO and CAO with the appropriate chief of mission (COM).
Commander, United States Special Operations Command	Commander, United States Special Operations Command provides GCCs with civil affairs (CA) from assigned forces that are organized, trained, and equipped to plan and conduct CAO in support of GCCs missions.
Subordinate Joint Force Commanders	Subordinate joint force commanders (JFCs) implement CA plans and coordinate CAO with country teams, interagency partners, IGOs, NGOs, IPI, and HN or foreign nation (FN) military and civilian authorities.
CMO Forces and Capabilities	Commanders at all levels should not consider CMO the sole responsibility of special operations forces (SOF) or specifically CA and military information support (MIS) units. CA and MIS units usually form the nucleus for

CMO planning efforts; while others, such as, SOF, engineers, health service support, transportation, and military police and security forces, normally function as CMO enablers.

Organizing for CMO

CMO are often key enablers to successful joint operations. Some of the types of CMO organizations are: the civil-military operations directorate of a joint staff (J-9), joint civil-military operations task forces (JCMOTFs), CMOCs, and civil-military teams.

CMO Directorate of a Joint Staff (J-9)

J-9 builds relations with military and civilian organizations that influence operations or campaigns. The J-9 provides a conduit for information sharing, coordinating support requests and activities, compiling and analyzing relevant information, and performing analysis that supports the commander's assessment.

Joint CMO Task Force

JFCs may establish a **JCMOTF** when the scope of CMO requirements and activities are beyond the JFC's organic capability.

Civil-Military Operations Center

A **CMOC** is formed to provide a joint force forum for organizations which want to maintain their neutrality. The CMOC receives, validates, and coordinates requests for support from NGOs, IGOs, and the private sector. The CMOC then forwards these requests to the joint force for action.

Civil-Military Team

A **civil-military team** helps stabilize the operational environment (OE) in a province, district, state, or locality through its combined diplomatic, informational, military, and economic capabilities. It combines representatives from interagency (and perhaps multinational) partners into a cohesive unit capable of independently conducting operations to stabilize a part of the OE by enhancing the legitimacy and the effectiveness of the HN government.

Planning

The J-9 normally leads the CMO staff element and is an important asset in planning and coordinating CMO.

Joint planners should incorporate CMO into the deliberate and crisis action planning processes. In theater campaign planning, CMO enables eventual transition to civilian control after major operations. CMO planning normally conforms to five lines of effort: economic stability, infrastructure, public health and welfare, public education and information, and rule of law.

Planning Considerations	Joint force planners must understand national security policy and objectives, as well as national and theater military objectives. Planning considerations include:

- Administrative, logistic, and communications support requirements of CMO forces;

- The coordination of CMO requirements with other appropriate staff functions, interagency, intergovernmental organizations, nongovernmental organizations, host nation, and private sector; and

- Language, cultural, and social customs for the operational area.

Civil Affairs Forces and Civil Affairs Operations

CA specialize in indirect approaches in support of traditional warfare (e.g., stability operations), and irregular warfare.	CA forces conduct military engagement, humanitarian and civic assistance, and nation assistance to influence HN and FN populations. CA forces assess impacts of the population and culture on military operations; assess impact of military operations on the population and culture; and facilitate interorganizational coordination.
CA Responsibilities	CA joint responsibilities include plan, coordinate, conduct, and assess CAO, and support building partnership capability.
Civil Affairs Operations	CAO are actions to coordinate with HN military and civilian agencies, other government departments and agencies, NGOs, or IGOs, to support US policy or the commander's assigned mission.

Coordination

Interorganizational coordination is an essential requirement for unified action.	The joint force and the country team should facilitate interorganizational coordination. The JFC, in coordination with the COM, should determine whether the CMOC can serve as the USG's primary interface for other government departments and agencies, IPI, IGOs, NGOs, and multinational forces.
Host Nation and Foreign Nation	CMO identifies resources, to include potential host-nation support and foreign nation support. CMO can also help

prevent unnecessary civilian hardship by advocating US and HN legal obligations and moral considerations.

Interagency Coordination

Organizations such as the joint interagency coordination group (JIACG) and CMOC support interorganizational coordination. The JIACG is an interagency staff group that establishes working relationships between civilian and military operational planners.

Intergovernmental Organizations and Nongovernmental Organizations

IGOs are created by a formal agreement (e.g., a treaty) between two or more governments on a global or regional basis for general or specialized purposes. IGOs and NGOs are essential to resolve and stabilize many humanitarian crises. The JFC should coordinate with IGOs and NGOs as early as possible.

The Private Sector

The private sector can assist the USG by sharing information, identifying risks, performing vulnerability assessments, assisting in contingency and crisis action planning, and providing other assistance as appropriate. CMO encourage individual businesses, trade associations, and other private sector organizations to foster dialogue with the US military and the HN government.

CONCLUSION

This publication provides joint doctrine for planning and conducting CMO by joint forces, employing civil affairs forces, conducting civil affairs operations, and coordinating with departments, agencies, or other organizations during the execution of CMO.

Intentionally Blank

CHAPTER I
INTRODUCTION

"The United States Government will make a sustained effort to engage civil society and citizens and facilitate increased connections among the American people and peoples around the world through efforts ranging from public service and educational exchanges, to increased commerce and private sector partnerships."

National Security Strategy, May 2010

1. General

a. **Strategic Aspects of Civil-Military Operations (CMO).** Joint force commanders (JFCs) should build mutual support and integrate with the other instruments of national power to accomplish national strategic objectives. Resolving national security issues in the dynamic strategic environment of the 21st century typically requires a range of diplomatic, informational, military, and economic solutions. Both threats and opportunities emanate from the civil sector of any society. Potential challenges to security, stability, and peace include ethnic and religious conflict; cultural and socioeconomic friction; terrorism and insurgencies; the proliferation of weapons of mass destruction (WMD); international organized crime; incidental and deliberate population migration; environmental security; infectious diseases; and increasing competition for, or exploitation of, dwindling natural resources. These challenges can be addressed through the integration and comprehensive use of intergovernmental organizations (IGOs), national and local governments, and nongovernmental and private sector organizations, which have proliferated in number, variety, and capability. Recent policy initiatives, national security directives, military strategies, and evolving military doctrine reflect a growing appreciation of the need to leverage more nonmilitary tools and elements of the instruments of national power, such as interagency partners and private sector, in order to build a more holistic and balanced strategy. National Security Presidential Directive (NSPD)-44, *Management of Interagency Efforts Concerning Reconstruction and Stabilization,* for example, tasks the Department of State (DOS) to lead interagency coordination, planning, and civil response for reconstruction and stabilization to coordinate and strengthen efforts of the United States Government (USG) to prepare, plan, and conduct reconstruction and stabilization assistance and related activities in a range of situations that require the response capabilities of multiple USG entities and to harmonize such efforts with US military plans and operations. Department of Defense Instruction (DODI) 3000.05, *Stability Operations*, notes, "Integrated civilian and military efforts are essential to the conduct of successful stability operations." At the strategic, operational, and tactical levels of war, and during all military operations, CMO are essential to the military instrument to coordinate the integration of military and nonmilitary instruments of national power, particularly in support of stability, counterinsurgency (COIN), and other operations dealing with asymmetric and irregular threats. Because they may permeate other aspects of national security and military strategy for an operation or campaign, CMO are inherently strategic in nature and key to achieving national security objectives.

(1) Well designed CMO should be holistic, cumulative, integrative, and synergistic. CMO foster cooperation between military forces, the host nation (HN), and interorganizational partners by building trust and mutual understanding to facilitate civil-military transition, minimize costs and risks, and mitigate threats and exploit opportunities. CMO promote unity of effort and facilitate transition from military to civil authority. CMO also reduce friction in civil-military relationships to make US and allied decision-making processes faster than adversaries such as insurgents, transnational criminal enterprises, and terrorist organizations. Properly planned and monitored CMO synchronize the instruments of national power to produce greater efficiency, better understanding of assessment tools, faster responses, improved accountability, and more sustainable operations after transition.

(2) Detailed analysis of indigenous populations and cultures is essential to design and plan effective CMO. Understanding local population and culture enables effective engagement. Individuals and units tasked with CMO will likely be immersed in an indigenous culture. These units should remain adaptive and attuned to socio-culturally relevant aspects of the operational environment (OE).

(3) CMO typically coordinate the efforts of joint, interagency, and multinational organizations. CMO's coordinating and civil information management (CIM) functions build unity of effort and enable unified action.

(4) At all levels, CMO use negotiation, mediation, collaboration, consensus, and relationship building to create conditions for success.

(5) JFCs integrate civil affairs (CA) forces with other military forces (e.g., maneuver, health service, military police [MP], engineer, transportation, and special operations forces [SOF]), to work alongside HN agencies, military, and security forces (e.g., national, border, and local police) as well as the indigenous populations and institutions (IPI). Through interorganizational coordination, the JFC may enable unified action that includes other USG departments and agencies, IGOs, nongovernmental organizations (NGOs), HNs, foreign nations (FNs), and the private sector.

For more details on the interagency community, IPI, HNs, IGOs, NGOs, and the private sector, refer to Chapter V, "Coordination," and Joint Publication (JP) 3-08, Interorganizational Coordination During Joint Operations. *Collectively, the above terms often are referred to as "stakeholders."*

b. **CMO.** CMO are the activities of a commander performed by designated CA or other military forces that establish, maintain, influence, or exploit relationships between military forces and IPI, by directly supporting the attainment of objectives relating to the reestablishment or maintenance of stability within a region or HN. CMO may include military forces conducting activities and functions of the local, regional, or national government. These activities may occur prior to, during, or subsequent to other military actions. They may also occur, if directed, in the absence of other military operations. CMO may be performed by designated CA forces, other military forces, or a combination of CA and other forces, and are conducted across the range of military operations as depicted in Figure I-1.

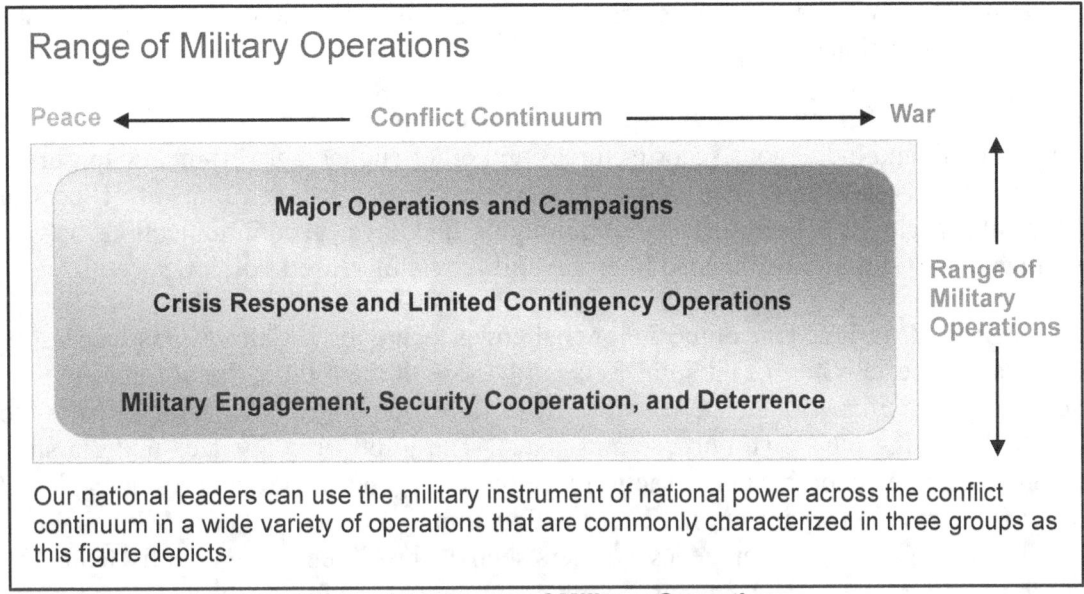

Figure I-1. Range of Military Operations

(1) CMO contribute to missions within many operational areas by synchronizing and building synergy between multiple players and entities contributing to the stabilization of the HN.

(2) CMO help disseminate relevant messages and themes to local leaders and the HN population.

(3) CMO also provide feedback to information operations (IO) as the assessments reveal sentiments of targeted HN populations or organizations.

c. **Authority to Conduct CMO**

(1) Authority to conduct CMO can be derived from joint operations, an international cooperative agreement, or an agreement between the USG or appropriate military commander and the government of the area or country in which US forces may be employed. A commander's authority to undertake CMO derives from Presidential or Secretary of Defense (SecDef) decisions. US strategic objectives, US policy, and relations between the HN government and the USG also influence the authority to conduct CMO.

(2) The law of war requires occupying powers to restore public order and safety while respecting, to the extent possible, the laws of the occupied country; and to establish a civil administration and to control or conduct governmental matters during and after hostilities. International law determines when a territory or a region is actually under the authority of an occupying force, which generally follows the cessation of hostilities. Occupation is a question of fact based on the ability of the occupying force to render the occupied government incapable of exercising public authority or, in the absence of a local government, an ungoverned area. However, mere presence of foreign forces in a nation does not confer occupation rights or responsibilities on that force. Foreign forces present in a

sovereign state by consent exercise rights and responsibilities arising from established accords or international agreements.

d. **Liaison.** Effective CMO require extensive liaison and coordination among US, multinational, and indigenous security forces and other engaged government departments and agencies as well as NGOs, IGOs, IPI, or the private sector. Liaison officers are commonly employed to establish close, continuous, and physical communications between organizations resulting in enhanced interoperability and increased mission success.

e. **Unified Action.** One of the major challenges facing the JFC in CMO is successfully coordinating the activities of the joint force with those of the multinational forces (MNFs) and multiple civilian organizations within the joint operations area (JOA), with each potentially having their own purpose and goals. The joint force operates under a single responsible commander, but unified action requires interagency coordination among all USG participants and interorganizational coordination among all participants. CMO should be closely coordinated with interagency partners such as the US embassy country team. The JFC should coordinate CMO amongst components, supporting forces, the country team, and HN. This is particularly important for lethal operations involving tactical air support or indirect fires. CMO operations at the tactical, operational, and strategic levels should be nested to ensure unity of effort. Effective planning and coordination for unified action should result in unity of effort during execution.

f. **Civilian-Military Relations. Civilian-military relations are normally the responsibility of the JFC. CMO have proven essential for those relations and typically facilitate accomplishment of the commander's overall mission.** Adversaries may use irregular warfare (IW) to avoid direct confrontation with the US. They may target civilian populations instead of military forces. This erodes distinction between civilian and military institutions, infrastructures, and systems; military and civilian "dual use" infrastructures are becoming more prevalent. Cities and social and cultural hubs are often centers of gravity (COGs) or decisive points rather than military forces or geographic locations. As more people and the influence of their greater numbers migrate to densely populated urban areas, the joint force is more likely to be operating in urban areas than in remote locations. Consequently, **CMO should be considered in the planning and execution of military operations.**

2. Civil-Military Operations and Levels of War

a. The levels of war are doctrinal perspectives that clarify the links between strategic objectives and tactical actions. The national strategic objectives facilitate theater strategic planning. Military strategy, derived from policy, is the basis for all operations (see JP 3-0, *Joint Operations*). CMO are applicable at the strategic, operational, and tactical levels of war. Specific actions at one level of war may affect all three levels simultaneously but with different effects at each level. CMO guidance should therefore include higher headquarters objectives and end states presented by USG policy and guidance. Individuals and units conducting CMO must understand the interrelationships of the levels of war.

b. Engaged civilian organizations likely will be more concerned with a predetermined agenda and not distinguish between the various levels of war. NGO or IGO members who communicate with US forces may report conversations to foreign officials at the highest level, who may then discuss them directly with the USG officials. Misperceptions of CMO actions by nonmilitary agencies can cause a commander to be distracted from the mission. Most civilian agencies are not organized with distinct operational, tactical, or strategic levels. NGO and IGO representatives collocated with forward-deployed joint forces often do not have the authority to make decisions that may change their original mission. As such, it is important that JFCs conducting CMO should understand the civilian participant's organizational and hierarchical relationships as they relate to decision making. This will help clarify working relationships and reduce friction with all parties concerned.

c. CMO are conducted at multiple levels. The effort at each level may be focused on different objectives, but the activities should be mutually supporting.

(1) **Strategic.** At the strategic level, CMO focus on larger and long-term issues that may be part of a Department of Defense (DOD) global campaign, or USG reconstruction, economic development initiatives, and stability operations in failing or recovering nations. CMO are a component of a geographic combatant commander's (GCC's) theater security cooperation guidance within the theater campaign plan (TCP). As such, the GCC's TCP objectives must align with national strategic objectives.

(2) **Operational**

(a) At the operational level, CMO integrate and synchronize interagency, IGO and NGO activities with joint force operations. Interagency, IGO, and NGO activities generally support security cooperation and feature programs to build relationships and mitigate the need for military force. Consequently, CMO focus on immediate or near-term issues such as health service infrastructure; movement, feeding, and sheltering of dislocated civilians (DCs); police and security programs; promoting government legitimacy; and coordination for CMO support to tactical commanders.

(b) Joint force planners and interagency partners should identify civil-military objectives early in the planning process. CMO are integrated into plans and operations through interagency coordination, multinational partnerships, and coordination with IGOs and NGOs. Coordination of CMO for current and future operations is conducted at the operational level. Information is valuable to interorganizational coordination, to efficiently and effectively marshall and distribute resources (to include funding), and to assess success in an OE where success may not be measured by traditional operational indicators. Information management (IM) enables CMO for operational commanders and facilitates the required interorganizational coordination necessary.

(3) **Tactical.** Often, a civil-military team or civil-military operations center (CMOC) may facilitate tactical-level CMO among the military, the local populace, NGOs, and IGOs. Commanders derive tactical-level CMO from the core tasks of support to civil administration (SCA), populace and resources control (PRC), foreign humanitarian assistance (FHA), nation assistance (NA), and CIM. Tactical-level CMO normally are more

sharply focused and have more immediate effects. Often, a civilian-military team or CMOC will facilitate these actions between the military, the local populace, and NGOs/IGOs. During certain contingency operations, the Secretary of State and SecDef will integrate stabilization and reconstruction contingency plans with military contingency plans and will develop a general framework for fully coordinating stabilization and reconstruction activities and military operations at all levels where appropriate. The DOS Bureau of Conflict and Stabilization is tasked to implement policy requirements from NSPD-44, *Management of Interagency Efforts Concerning Reconstruction and Stabilization.* This could provide a framework at the national strategic level for stabilization and reconstruction planning and coordination. SecDef, through the Chairman of the Joint Chiefs of Staff (CJCS), provides direction to combatant commanders (CCDRs) and subordinate JFCs to implement joint operation planning for the NSPD-44, *Management of Interagency Efforts Concerning Reconstruction and Stabilization,* process.

d. Annex G (Civil Affairs) promulgates CMO requirements in a formal plan or operation order. CMO require coordination among CA, maneuver, health support, MP, engineer, transportation, and SOF. CMO involve cross-cutting activities across staff sections and subordinate units. Annex G identifies, consolidates, and deconflicts the activities of the various sections and units. Planning and coordination at lower echelons require significantly more details than discussed in annex G.

For more details concerning annex G (Civil Affairs), refer to Chairman of the Joint Chiefs of Staff Manual (CJCSM) 3130.03, Adaptive Planning and Execution (APEX) Planning Formats and Guidance.

e. Changes in the military or political situation, as well as natural or man-made disasters, can divert the joint force's main effort from CMO to combat operations. The JFC should identify early indicators and warnings of changes in the OE and allocate resources to monitor these changes in order to anticipate changes in force requirements. Branch and sequel planning and preventive action may mitigate disruption of CMO. Potential indicators are depicted in Figure I-2.

3. Components of Civil-Military Operations

CMO are conducted to establish, maintain, influence, or exploit relationships between military forces, governmental and nongovernmental organizations and authorities, and the civilian populace in a permissive, uncertain, or hostile operational area in order to facilitate military operations, to consolidate and achieve operational US objectives.

a. CMO include a range of activities that integrate civil and military actions for SCA, PRC, FHA, NA, and CIM. These activities are particularly suited to support the development of a country's material and human resources, or to assist the HN in achieving other national objectives. CMO are normally based on the desired level of civilian support, availability of resources, and potential issues with inadvertent interference by the local population.

Possible Escalation Indicators

- Political activities and movements
- Food or water shortages
- Outbreaks of disease
- Military setbacks
- Natural disasters
- Crop failures
- Fuel shortages
- Onset of seasonal changes (winter may exacerbate fuel and food shortages, for example)
- Police force and corrections system deterioration
- Judicial system shortcomings
- Insurgent attacks
- Sharp rise in crime
- Terrorist bombing
- Disruption of public utilities, e.g., water, power, sewage, and economic strife due to socioeconomic imbalance
- Increase in local government corruption

Figure I-2. Possible Escalation Indicators

(1) **SCA.** SCA helps continue or stabilize management by a governing body of a FN's civilian authorities by assisting an established government, or by supporting establishment of a transitional military or civilian authority over an occupied population until an indigenous civil government can be established. SCA consists of planning, coordinating, advising, or assisting the commander with those activities that reinforce or restore a civil administration that supports US and multinational objectives. SCA occurs most often during stability operations. Some SCA activities may be used during PRC, FHA, and NA.

(a) **Civil administration in friendly territory** includes advising friendly authorities and performing specific functions within the limits of authority and liability established by mutual agreements, or treaties and agreements administered under the authority of an IGO (e.g., United Nations [UN]).

(b) **Civil administration in occupied territory** encompasses the establishment of a temporary military government, as directed by SecDef, to exercise executive, legislative, and judicial authority over the populace of a territory that US forces have taken from an enemy by force of arms until a civil government can be established. This may be an unilateral USG effort, or USG acting under the authority of an IGO; or a multinational effort not under the auspices of an IGO.

(c) **Domestic and International Considerations.** SCA is tailored to the situation based on US law, HN law, international law (including the law of war), international treaties, agreements, and memoranda of understanding. To the fullest extent of the means available to it, the occupying force must maintain an orderly government in the occupied territory and must have, as its ultimate goal, the creation of a legitimate and effective civilian government. Subject to the military requirements, the JFC should avoid military activities likely to increase tensions in the occupied territory and conduct those likely to facilitate and accelerate a return to a civil administration. This is especially important in multiethnic, multiracial, or multicultural environments where one or more of the parties to a conflict will almost invariably see a chosen course of action (COA) as biased against them.

(2) **PRC**

(a) PRC consists of two distinct, yet linked, components: populace control and resources control.

<u>1</u>. **Populace control** provides security to people, mobilizes human resources, denies personnel to the enemy, and detects and reduces the effectiveness of enemy agents. Populace control measures include curfews, movement restrictions, travel permits, identification and registration cards, and voluntary resettlement. DC operations involve populace control that requires extensive planning and coordination among various military and civilian organizations.

<u>2</u>. **Resources control** regulates the movement or consumption of materiel resources, mobilizes materiel resources, and denies materiel to the enemy. Resources control measures include licensing, regulations or guidelines, checkpoints (e.g., roadblocks), ration controls, amnesty programs, and inspection of facilities.

(b) These controls normally are a responsibility of HN civilian governments. US forces may implement PRC when HN civilian authorities or agencies are unable or unwilling to. PRC are escalated during civilian or military emergencies. In a permissive environment, joint forces implement PRC measures with the consent of the local government. In a hostile environment, PRC measures are applied in accordance with international law and the law of war.

(c) Nonlethal weapons can reduce the probability of death or serious injury to the civilian populace while maintaining effective force protection (FP) measures. Commanders should evaluate the use of nonlethal weapons in operation plans.

For further guidance on nonlethal weapons, see Department of Defense Directive (DODD) 3000.3, Policy for Non-Lethal Weapons.

(3) **FHA.** FHA operations are conducted outside the US and its territories, normally in support of the United States Agency for International Development (USAID) or DOS, and include programs conducted to relieve or reduce the results of natural or man-made disasters or other conditions, such as disease, hunger, or privation that might present a serious threat to life or that can result in great damage to or loss of property. FHA provided

by US forces is limited in scope and duration and is designed to supplement or complement the efforts of the HN civil authorities or agencies that may have the primary responsibility for providing assistance.

For further detail concerning FHA, refer to JP 3-29, Foreign Humanitarian Assistance, *and DODD 5100.46,* Foreign Disaster Relief (FDR).

(4) **NA.** NA is assistance rendered to a nation by US forces within that nation's territory based on mutual agreement. NA promotes stability, sustainable development, and establishes HN internal institutions responsive to the populace. NA is military engagement, security cooperation, and deterrence operations that enhance the CCDR's shaping and deterrence efforts. All NA actions are integrated with the chief of mission's (COM's) mission resource request. The goal is to promote long-term regional stability. NA programs often include, but are not limited to, security assistance, foreign internal defense (FID), other Title 10, United States Code (USC) programs and activities performed on a reimbursable basis by USG departments and agencies or IGOs.

(a) Security cooperation is the means by which DOD encourages and enables countries and organizations to work with the US to achieve strategic goals.

(b) FID programs are the diplomatic, economic, informational, and military support to another nation which assists its fight against subversion, lawlessness, and insurgency. US military involvement in FID includes indirect support, direct support, and combat operations.

<u>1</u>. Military operations related to FID are support to COIN, combating terrorism, peace operations (PO), DOD support to counterdrug operations, and FHA.

<u>2</u>. FID operations can help FNs control subversion, lawlessness, and insurgency.

For further detail in regard to FID and security assistance, refer to JP 3-22, Foreign Internal Defense.

(c) Other Title 10, USC, programs:

<u>1</u>. Section 401, Humanitarian and Civic Assistance (HCA) Provided in Conjunction with Military Operations. In contrast to FHA, US Armed Forces may provide HCA in conjunction with authorized military operations. HCA programs generally encompass planned activities and are limited by law to the following: medical, surgical, dental, and veterinary care provided in areas of the country that are rural or are underserved by medical, surgical, dental, and veterinary professionals, respectively, including education, training, and technical assistance related to the care provided; construction of rudimentary surface transportation systems; well drilling and construction of basic sanitation facilities; and rudimentary construction and repair of public facilities. The assistance provided must promote the security interests of both the US and the country in which the activities are to be carried out; and the specific operational readiness skills of the members of the US forces

participating in the activities. HCA activities must complement but not duplicate any other form of social or economic assistance provided by the US.

2. Section 402, Transportation of Humanitarian Relief Supplies to Foreign Countries. Under Title 10, USC, Section 402, SecDef may authorize the transport to any country, without charge, supplies furnished by nongovernmental sources intended for humanitarian assistance (HA). Transport is permitted only on a space-available basis. Supplies may be distributed by USG departments and agencies, foreign governments, international organizations, or nonprofit relief organizations. Supplies may not be distributed (directly or indirectly) to any individual, group, or organization engaged in military or paramilitary activities.

3. Section 404, Foreign Disaster Assistance. Under Title 10, USC, Section 404, the President may direct SecDef to provide disaster assistance outside the United States in response to man-made or natural disasters when necessary to prevent the loss of human life or serious harm to the environment. Assistance under Title 10, USC, Section 404, may include transportation, supplies, services, and equipment.

4. Section 407, Humanitarian Demining Assistance and Stockpiled Conventional Munitions Assistance: Authority and Limitations. Subject to regulations issued by SecDef, the Secretaries of the Military Departments are authorized by Title 10, USC, Section 407, to undertake humanitarian demining assistance activities and stockpiled conventional munitions assistance in foreign countries. The assistance provided must promote either the security interests of both the US and the country in which the activities are to be carried out; or the specific operational readiness skills of the members of the US Armed Forces participating in the activities. Humanitarian demining assistance activities and stockpiled conventional munitions assistance must complement but not duplicate any other form of social or economic assistance provided by the US. SecDef must ensure that no member of the US Armed Forces, while providing humanitarian demining assistance or stockpiled conventional munitions assistance, engages in the physical detection, lifting, or destroying of landmines or other explosive remnants of war, or stockpiled conventional munitions assistance (unless the member does so for the concurrent purpose of supporting a US military operation); or provides such assistance as part of a military operation that does not involve the armed forces.

For further details concerning humanitarian demining, refer to JP3-15, Barriers, Obstacles, and Mine Warfare for Joint Operations.

5. Section 2557, Excess Nonlethal Supplies: Humanitarian Relief. SecDef may make any DOD nonlethal excess supplies available for humanitarian relief purposes. Excess supplies furnished under this authority are transferred to DOS, which is responsible for distributing the supplies. Nonlethal excess supplies means property that is excess under DOD regulations and is not a weapon, ammunition, or other equipment or material designed to inflict serious bodily harm or death.

<u>6.</u> Section 2561, Humanitarian Assistance (HA). To the extent provided in defense authorization acts, funds appropriated to DOD for HA shall be used to transport humanitarian relief and for other humanitarian purposes worldwide.

<u>7.</u> Section 166a, Combatant Commands: Funding Through the Chairman of the Joint Chiefs of Staff. Military civic action (MCA) programs offer the JFC an opportunity to improve the HN infrastructure and the living conditions of the local populace while enhancing the legitimacy of the HN government. These programs use predominantly indigenous military forces in such fields as education, training, public works, agriculture, transportation, communications, health, sanitation, and other areas to improve HN economic and social development. These programs can have excellent long-term benefits for the HN by enhancing the effectiveness of the host government by developing needed skills and by enhancing the legitimacy of the host government by showing the people that their government is capable of meeting the population's basic needs. MCA programs can help gain the HN military public acceptance, which is especially important in stability and COIN operations with contentious human rights issues. MCA can also address root causes of civilian unrest through economic and social development services. Joint forces may supervise and advise during MCA, but the HN military should lead the visible effort. MCA projects require interagency cooperation, coordination, and monitoring to succeed. The JFC and staff should be aware of legal and financial limitations. MCA is similar to CMO except that in MCA, HN, or FN military or government personnel perform tasks that are visible to the indigenous population to garner popular support while US personnel provide training and advice.

For further detail relating to MCA, refer to JP 3-22, Foreign Internal Defense.

<u>8.</u> Section 168, Military-to-Military Contacts and Comparable Activities. SecDef is the program authority for the conduct of military-to-military activities. Military-to-military contacts generally promote a democratic orientation for nation partners' defense and security establishments. Examples of these activities include military liaison teams; exchanges of military and defense civilian personnel between DOD and the defense ministries of foreign governments; seminars and conferences held primarily in a theater of operations; and exchanges of military personnel between individual units of US forces and units of foreign armed forces.

Note: Military-to-military contacts must be approved by DOS.

(5) **CIM.** The focus of civil affairs operations (CAO) is to enable commanders to engage the civil component of the OE. CIM is one of the five CA core tasks. Rarely conducted in the absence of other CA core tasks, CIM focuses on collecting, collating, processing, analyzing, producing, and dissemination of relevant civil information to maintain influence or exploit relations between military forces, governmental and NGOs, and the civil population within any operational area. Analysis of civil information is at the core of CIM. Analysis is the sifting of information for patterns and indicators of past behavior's or ideas that might possess predictive value and application. Analysis molds information into a usable product for the commander and staff. CMO practitioners must direct analytical efforts to answer the civil unknowns in the common operational picture (COP) rather than

exhaustively refining data. Analysis of civil information is similar to the normal red team-blue team analysis process, but instead focuses on identifying mission variables; identifying operational variables; identifying COGs; identifying trends; conducting proactive analysis; and identifying civil vulnerabilities. Analysis of civil information must be packaged into easily disseminated forms structured so as to inform the commanders decision cycle. The CIM process ensures COM products and services are relevant, accurate, timely, and useable by commanders and decision makers. Products of civil information analysis are: layered geospatial information; civil information for the COP; COGs; civil consideration products; answers to request for information; reported priority intelligence requirements (PIRs); updates to ongoing CAO assessments, area studies, and running estimates. CIM core analytical efforts must allow commanders and decision makers to "see the data" via link analysis; civil consideration analysis; systems analysis; trend analysis. The CIM analytical tools may include stability matrices; nodal analysis charts; link analysis charts; geospatial analysis; and civil consideration overlay. The core analytical function of CIM informs the commander's decision cycle by providing civil information. CIM provides a prioritized, structured effort to support the commander's collection plan, provides input into building the civil layer of the COP, informs the joint targeting process/restricted target list, and contributes to COG analysis. The end state of CIM is to facilitate the fusion of civil information (green and white) with operations and intelligence (O&I). The end state of CIM is to better allow the commander to understand the OE. CIM is the process through which a commander communicates with partners outside of the military chain of command. CIM provides the commander situational understanding and knowledge of the civil component of the OE through a formal data management process. CIM enables the commander to disseminate raw and analyzed civil information to both military and nonmilitary partners.

(a) Commanders share information with partners to build legitimacy through transparency with the local, national, and international organizations; accomplish common goals; and gain comparative advantage through IPI capabilities.

(b) CIM extends the commander's operational reach through IPI resources and actions; accelerates transition to a civil government by using existing civil infrastructure and institutions; and provides insight on metrics not captured by organic assets.

(c) CIM can enable HN governments and the NGO and IGO communities. Shared civil information can enable cooperation between IGOs, NGOs, and MNFs to efficiently use limited resources.

(d) Subordinate JFCs synchronize their operations directly with the activities and operations of other military forces and nonmilitary organizations in their operational area. CIM provides a collaborative information environment through a virtual aggregation of individuals, organizations, systems, infrastructure, and processes which provides data and information to plan, execute, and assess CAO in support of CMO. It will enable CA leaders to make more informed recommendations to the supported commander.

See Appendix C, "Civil Information Management," for more details on CIM.

b. **CMO in Joint Operations. CMO may occur in any phase of military operations.** CMO can be broadly separated into population-centric actions and support to civil actions, though at times these operations can become mixed depending upon the OE.

(1) **CMO Studies.** CMO planners should forecast and continuously reevaluate CMO requirements by analyzing the mission to determine specific tasks. This includes establishing guidance for the specific CMO tasks and developing estimates of the situation to include area studies. In denied areas, CMO planners use intelligence products to access, gather, and validate information for area or functional oriented studies. Planners should consider their knowledge of CMO, geographic areas of specialization, language qualifications, civil sector functional technical expertise, and contacts with IPI. This will allow for timely and critical information on the civilian capabilities and resources in the operational area. Civilian contacts may provide more extensive insight than information collected through intelligence channels, but CMO planners should validate all critical information and assumptions through intelligence capabilities. CA area studies and area assessments provide operational analysis of the civil component of the OE.

(a) CMO tasks vary throughout operation phases. Although JFCs determine the number and actual phases used during a campaign or operation, use of the phases provides a flexible model to arrange CMO. These activities may be performed by CA personnel, other military forces, or combination.

<u>1</u>. **Phase 0—Shape.** During the implementation of the CCDR's security cooperation planning objectives CMO can mitigate the need for other military operations in response to a crisis. CA support FID and contribute to contingency and crisis action planning. In a crisis, CA forces working with HNs, regional partners, and IPI can shape the environment. Shaping operations can include regional conferences to bring together multiple factions with competing concerns and goals, economic agreements designed to build interdependency, or regional aid packages to enhance stability.

<u>2</u>. **Phase I—Deter.** CMO should be integrated with flexible deterrent options to generate maximum strategic or operational effect. CMO in the deter phase builds on activities from the shape phase. CA forces support NA, SA, FID, and PO. CA can also conduct area studies and update area assessments to identify potential civil sector and civilian COGs.

<u>3</u>. **Phase II—Seize the Initiative.** During this phase, CMO are conducted to gain access to theater infrastructure and to expand friendly freedom of action in support of JFC operations. CMO are designed to minimize civil-military friction and support friendly political-military objectives.

<u>4</u>. **Phase III—Dominate.** CMO also help minimize HN civilian interface with joint operations so that collateral damage to IPI from offensive, defensive, or stability operations is limited. Limiting collateral damage may reduce the duration and intensity of combat and stability operations. Stability operations are conducted as needed to ensure a smooth transition to the next phase, relieve suffering, and set conditions for civil-military transition.

        5. **Phase IV—Stabilize.** The stabilize phase is required when there is no fully functional, legitimate civil governing authority. The joint force may be required to perform limited local governance, integrate the efforts of other supporting or contributing multinational, IGO, NGO, or USG department and agency participants until legitimate local entities are functioning. This phase can be marked by transition from sustained combat operations to stability operations. As this occurs, CMO facilitate humanitarian relief, civil order, and restoration of public services as fighting subsides. Throughout this segment, the JFC continuously assesses whether current operations enable transfer of overall regional authority to a legitimate civil entity, which marks the end of the phase.

        6. **Phase V—Enable Civil Authority.** This phase is predominantly characterized by joint force support to legitimate civil governance in the operational area. This includes coordination of CMO with interagency, multinational, IPI, IGO, and NGO participants; establishing and assessing measures of effectiveness (MOEs) and measures of performance (MOPs); and favorably influencing the attitude of the HN population regarding both the US and the local civil authority's objectives. Figure I-3 illustrates possible CMO MOPs and MOEs.

For more details concerning the phasing model, refer to JP 3-0, Joint Operations.

Possible Measures of Performance and Measures of Effectiveness for Civil-Military Operations

Measures of Performance

- Shape: foreign humanitarian assistance supplied, quick impact projects.
- Deter: levels of violent/disruptive events.
- Seize the Initiative: integration with host nation civil-military authorities, host nation government, integration with local populace.
- Dominate: decrease in hostilities, decrease in collateral damage/deaths, injuries.
- Stabilize: humanitarian assistance relief, restoration of services, repair/rebuilding projects.
- Enable Civil Authority: train/equip law enforcement and military, political elections, mentoring of government officials.

Measures of Effectiveness

- Shape: perception by host nation government and host nation populace, reduction of turmoil, return to pre-event levels.
- Deter: restoration of pre-event civil activities.
- Seize the Initiative: perception that host nation government and civil-military authorities are legitimate/credible and that United States Government (USG) intervention is welcome.
- Dominate: host nation government lead and legitimacy, USG supporting role is unhindered and unchallenged.
- Stabilize: self-sufficiency/stability at pre-event levels or better.
- Enable Civil Authority: self-sufficient/legitimate military and law enforcement, legitimate/unquestioned political elections, legitimate government.

Figure I-3. Possible Measures of Performance and Measures of Effectiveness for Civil-Military Operations

---

(a) DC operations are designed to minimize civil-military friction, reduce civilian casualties, alleviate human suffering, and control DC movements.

(b) CMO coordinates with civilian agencies to implement measures to locate and identify population centers. CMO also coordinate with civilian agencies to create, restore, and maintain public order. CMO coordinate resources (e.g., labor, supplies, and facilities). CMO coordinate immediate life sustaining services to civilians in the operational area(s) and assist with planning for disease control measures to protect joint forces.

(c) CMO assets may designate routes and facilities for DCs to minimize their contact with forces engaged in combat.

(d) CMO may help contribute to logistics operations. CMO planners can help logistic planners identify available goods and services by using their contacts within the civilian sector.

(e) Even limited military operations such as raids and strikes may significantly affect the civil environment. CMO implications for most of these operations depend on the mission scope, national strategic end state, and the characteristics of the civil sector in the operational area. CMO activities in support of joint operations include:

<u>1</u>. **COIN.** COIN operations are comprehensive civilian and military efforts taken to simultaneously defeat and contain insurgency and address its root causes. CMO support to COIN operations includes using military capabilities to perform traditionally civilian activities to help HN or FN deprive insurgents of popular support. CMO activities combine military-joint operations with diplomatic, political, economic, and informational initiatives of the HN and engaged interorganizational partners to foster stability. The principle goal of CMO in COIN operations or FID is to isolate the insurgents from the populace, thus depriving them of recruits, resources, intelligence, and credibility.

<u>2</u>. **Security Assistance.** CMO support to security assistance can include training foreign military forces in CMO and civil-military relations. CMO support training that is beyond the capability of in-country US military assistance elements. The security cooperation planning should synchronize CMO planning and CA forces with the other security assistance capabilities.

<u>3</u>. **PO.** PO are normally multiagency and multinational contingencies involving all instruments of national power, and may include international humanitarian and reconstruction efforts. CMO foster a cooperative relationship between the military forces, civilian organizations, and the governments and populations in the operational area.

<u>4</u>. **Noncombatant Evacuation Operation (NEO).** CMO support to NEO is designed to limit local national interference with evacuation operations, maintain close liaison with embassy officials to facilitate effective interagency coordination, obtain civil or indigenous support for the NEO, help DOS identify US citizens and others to be evacuated, and help embassy personnel receive, screen, process, and debrief evacuees.

(f) **Stability Operations.** Stability Operations are designed to maintain or reestablish a safe and secure environment and provide essential governmental services, emergency infrastructure reconstruction, or humanitarian relief. Stability operations support USG plans for reconstruction and development operations and likely will be conducted in coordination with and in support of HN authorities, other USG departments and agencies, IGOs, and NGOs.

1. Operation plans should balance offensive and defensive operations and stability operations in all phases. Planning for stability operations should begin when the joint operation planning process (JOPP) is initiated. Even during combat operations to the joint force may be required to establish or restore security and provide humanitarian relief.

2. Initial CMO will likely secure and safeguard the populace, reestablish civil law and order, protect and repair critical infrastructure, and restore public services. US military forces should be prepared to accomplish these tasks when indigenous civil, USG, multinational or international capacity cannot. US military forces may also support legitimate civil authority.

3. US forces robust logistic and command and control (C2) capabilities are often essential to stability operations. Normally other agencies such as DOS or USAID are responsible for USG objectives, but lack logistic and C2 capabilities. Because of the imbalance between capability and responsibility, stability operations will likely support, or transition support to, US diplomatic, IGO, or HN efforts. Military forces support the lead agency. US forces should be prepared to operate in integrated civilian-military teams that could include representatives from IPI, IGOs, NGOs, and members of the private sector.

4. Peace building's five mission sectors are security; HA and social well-being; justice and reconciliation; governance and participation; and economic stabilization and infrastructure. Commanders should conduct mission analysis in collaboration with national and intergovernmental agencies for each peace building sector and understand the impact of each sector on the others. For greater details see JP 3-07.3, *Peace Operations.*

4. Civil-Military Operations, Civil Affairs, and Unified Action

a. In carrying out their CMO responsibilities, commanders use CAO. The relationship between CMO and CAO is best considered within the broad context of unified action that involves the synchronization, coordination, or integration of the activities of governmental and nongovernmental entities with military operations to achieve unity of effort. JFCs seek this synergy by several means, one of the more prominent being through the conduct of CMO that bring together the activities of joint forces and MNFs and nonmilitary organizations to achieve common objectives. This relationship is depicted in Figure I-4.

(1) There are six CA functional specialty areas: rule of law, economic stability, governance, public health and welfare, infrastructure, and public education and information. All six functional specialties are interrelated, and specialists must often work together. See Figure I-5.

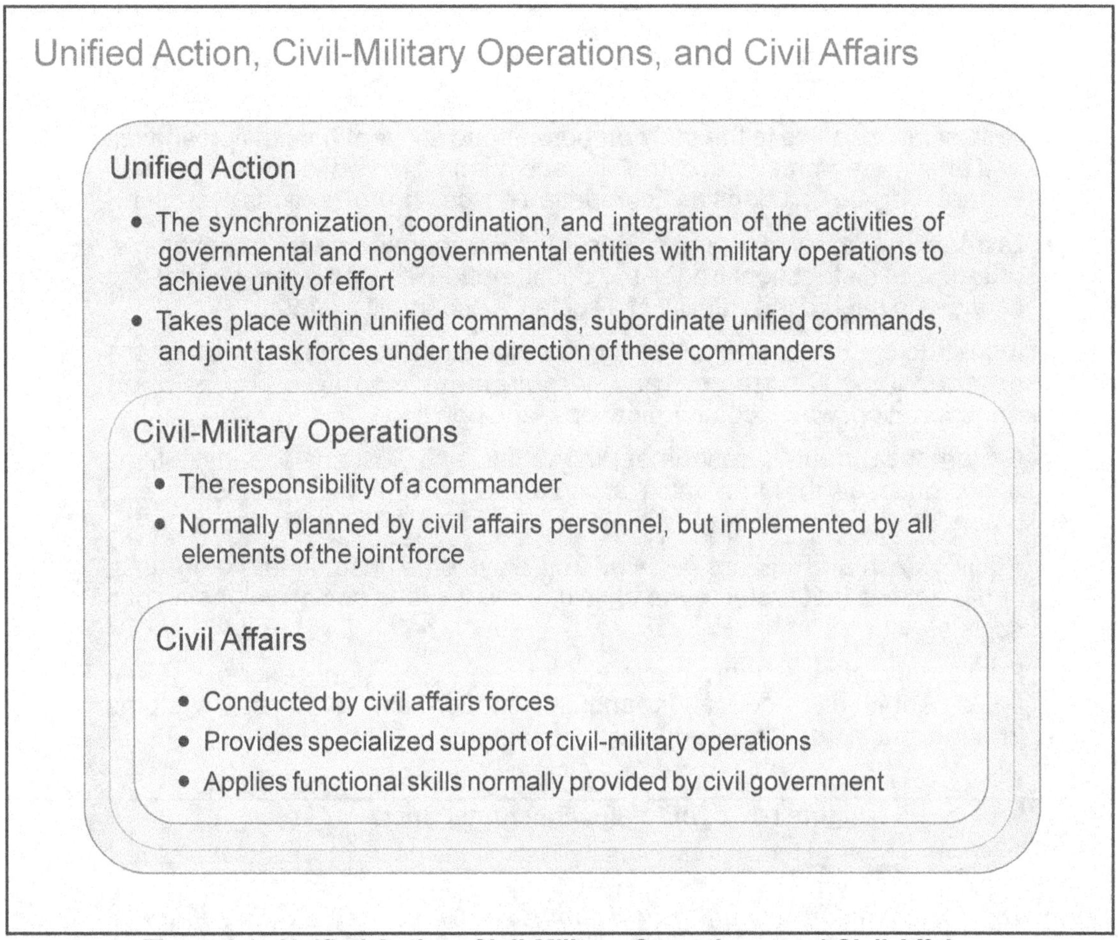

Unified Action, Civil-Military Operations, and Civil Affairs

Unified Action

- The synchronization, coordination, and integration of the activities of governmental and nongovernmental entities with military operations to achieve unity of effort
- Takes place within unified commands, subordinate unified commands, and joint task forces under the direction of these commanders

Civil-Military Operations

- The responsibility of a commander
- Normally planned by civil affairs personnel, but implemented by all elements of the joint force

Civil Affairs

- Conducted by civil affairs forces
- Provides specialized support of civil-military operations
- Applies functional skills normally provided by civil government

Figure I-4. Unified Action, Civil-Military Operations, and Civil Affairs

(2) CA functional specialists advise and assist the commander and can assist or direct subordinate civilian counterparts. These functional specialists should be employed to provide analysis in their specialty area that supports planning of interagency efforts or HN efforts, and in a general support role to joint force components requiring such capabilities.

b. GCCs can establish civil-military operations directorate of a joint staff (J-9) to plan, coordinate, conduct, and assess CMO. While CA forces are organized, trained, and equipped specifically to support CMO, other joint forces supporting CMO include SOF, military information support (MIS), legal support, public affairs (PA), engineer, transportation, health support personnel, MP, security forces, and maneuver units.

c. The J-9 develops CMO staff estimates and recommends JFC interorganizational coordination.

d. CAO are planned, executed, and assessed by CA forces due to the complexities and demands for specialized capabilities associated with activities normally the responsibility of indigenous civil governments or authorities. **While all CAO support CMO, they remain a distinct CMO element.**

Civil Affairs Functional Specialty Areas

- Rule of law pertains to the fair, competent, and efficient application and fair and effective enforcement of the civil and criminal laws of a society through impartial legal institutions and competent police and corrections systems.

- Economic stability pertains to the efficient management (for example, production, distribution, trade, and consumption) of resources, goods, and services to ensure the viability of a society's economic system.

- Infrastructure pertains to the design, construction, and maintenance of the organizations, systems, and architecture required to support transportation, water, communications, and power.

- Governance creates, resources, manages, and sustains the institutions and processes through which a society is governed, is protected, and prospers.

- Public health and welfare pertains to the systems, institutions, programs, and practices that promote the physical, mental, and social well-being of a society.

- Public education and information pertain to the design, resourcing, and implementation of education and information programs and systems through media and formal education institutions.

Figure I-5. Civil Affairs Functional Specialty Areas

For more information on civil affair operations, see Chapter IV, "Civil Affairs Forces and Civil Affairs Operations."

CHAPTER II
ORGANIZATION AND COMMAND RELATIONSHIPS
FOR CIVIL-MILITARY OPERATIONS

> *"One of the most important lessons of the wars in Iraq and Afghanistan is that military success is not sufficient to win: economic development, institution building and the rule of law, promoting internal reconciliation, good governance, providing basic services to the people, training and equipping indigenous military and police forces, strategic communications, and more—these, along with security, are essential ingredients for long-term success."*
>
> **Secretary of Defense Robert M. Gates**
> **Landon Lecture, Kansas State University**
> **26 November 2007**

1. General

CMO are JFC activities designed to establish and maintain relations with civil authorities, the general population, and other organizations. JFC plans and directs CMO in their operational areas. Maintaining military-to-civil relations and open communications with IGOs, NGOs, and selected elements of the private sector is integral to CMO.

a. The principles of effective C2 and staff organizational concepts apply to CMO just as they do for any other military operation.

b. CMO help integrate instruments of national power, minimize civil-military friction, maximize support for operations, and identify the commander's legal responsibilities and potential moral obligations to the civilian populations within the operational area.

2. Responsibilities

a. **The President or SecDef provide** policy guidance concerning civil-military interaction through the CJCS to the CCDR.

b. **Assistant SecDef for Special Operations and Low-Intensity Conflict:**

(1) Acts as the principal civilian advisor to SecDef and the Under Secretary of Defense for Policy (USD[P]) on the policy and planning for the use of CA within DOD.

(2) Supervises the formulation of plans and policy impacting DOD CAO.

(3) Provides policy advice, assistance, and coordination with other offices of Office of the Secretary of Defense (OSD) and DOD officials regarding CAO and the use of CA in their responsible areas.

(4) Acts as OSD point of contact for DOD:

(a) Coordinates CAO as they relate to the activities of interagency partners, IGOs, NGOs, IPI, other organizations, and the private sector, in accordance with applicable laws and regulations to plan and conduct CMO.

(b) Monitors interagency partner use of DOD forces for the conduct of CAO. SecDef should be contacted whenever questions arise with respect to legality or propriety of such use.

(5) Coordinates with OSD Director of Administration and Management to approve the detail of CA to duty with interagency partners.

(6) Reviews and coordinates requests for deployments for CA forces and making recommendations to the USD(P).

c. **CJCS:**

(1) Provides, as the principal military advisor to the President, the National Security Council (NSC), and SecDef, advice on the employment of CMO and CA forces and the conduct of CMO and CAO.

(2) Provides guidance to the supported CCDRs for the integration of CMO and CAO into military plans and operations, including security cooperation planning.

(3) Integrates agency and multinational partners into planning efforts as appropriate.

(4) Develops and promulgates joint doctrine for CMO to include CA, engineer, medical, security personnel, and other CMO supporting forces.

(5) Submits deployment orders for CA forces to the OSD in accordance with current DOD instructions for coordinating deployments.

d. **GCCs.** The GCCs provide regional coordination and direction to their subordinate commanders for the integration of CMO and CAO into military plans and operations. These activities are designed to:

(1) Support the goals and programs of other USG departments and agencies related to CMO and CAO consistent with missions and guidance issued by SecDef.

(2) Coordinate CMO and CAO with the appropriate COM.

(3) Synchronize CMO and CAO requirements within regional plans and security cooperation activities and other phase 0 (Shape) activities.

(4) **GCCs:**

(a) Plan, support, and conduct CMO and CAO. These activities shall be designed to:

1. Support national security policy and DOD goals and objectives.

2. Support the goals and programs of stakeholders through interaction as it relates to CMO and CAO missions and guidance issued by SecDef.

3. Support USG and DOD policy regarding respect for national sovereignty by coordinating with appropriate US embassies to establish HN agreements or arrangements with FNs that will be transited or within which joint forces will stage or operate. Information on existing agreements and arrangements with FNs can be found in the DOD *Foreign Clearance Guide,* and the DOD *Foreign Clearance Manual.* These publications provide information on requirements and restrictions for DOD personnel conducting temporary travel and aircraft over flight and landing in FNs around the world. The information is coordinated daily with DOS, US embassies, and combatant commands (CCMDs). Reference the Electronic Foreign Clearance Guide at https://www.fcg.pentagon.mil or http://www.fcg.pentagon.smil.mil for current copy of the DOD *Foreign Clearance Manual.*

(b) Assess the effectiveness of CMO executed as part of security cooperation planning and adjust activities as required.

(c) Assist the organizations having a part in CMO in working together to focus and synchronize their efforts in achieving CMO priorities in their area of responsibility (AOR).

e. **Commander, United States Special Operations Command (CDRUSSOCOM),** carries out responsibilities specified in subparagraph 2d(1) and:

(1) Provides GCCs with CA from assigned forces that are organized, trained, and equipped to plan and conduct CAO in support of GCCs missions.

(2) Provides education and individual training in planning and conducting CAO for DOD and non-DOD personnel.

(3) Assists in integrating CMO and CAO into joint strategy and doctrine under direction of the CJCS.

(4) Establishes prioritization and validate requirements for the deployment of assigned CA forces.

(5) Serves as the joint proponent for CA, including doctrine, combat development, and training.

f. The **Secretaries of the Military Departments**:

(1) Validate operational requirements for the deployment of assigned CA forces.

(2) Provide timely activation and mobilization of Reserve Component (RC) units.

(3) Assume DOD-wide responsibilities for specific CAO as directed by SecDef.

g. **The Secretaries of the Army and Navy**:

(1) Carry out the responsibilities specified in subparagraph 2f above.

(2) Recruit, train, organize, equip, and mobilize units and personnel to meet the CA requirements of the supported commander and provide CA forces requested by the other DOD components as directed by SecDef in accordance with the force levels, programs, plans, and missions approved by SecDef.

h. **Services**. Service Chiefs support interagency partners, the other Services, and multinational commanders and US CCDRs with forces, specialists, and Service-specific equipment to perform CMO. Additionally, the Service Chiefs:

(1) Support US policy and CCDR CA force requirements across the range of military operations.

(2) Direct their Service to cover CMO and CAO in Service planning.

i. **Subordinate JFCs**:

(1) Plan, integrate, and monitor the deployment, employment, sustainment, and redeployment of CA forces.

(2) Implement CA plans consistent with international law, the law of war, and US law and treaty obligations, and coordinate agreements and arrangements for en route transit of US military forces or materiel to support the operation.

(3) As directed, in accordance with law and formal agreements, control DCs, maintain order, prevent and treat disease, provide relief of civilian suffering, and protect and preserve property and other resources to achieve US military objectives.

(4) Educate assigned or attached personnel on relations with civilian authorities or HN population.

(5) Training and orientation for assigned or attached personnel on indigenous cultural and social attitudes and effects on military operations.

(6) Communicate civilian attitudes and needs to higher command and other government departments and agencies, IGOs, NGOs, IPI, and the private sector.

(7) Employ CMO and CA forces to identify and coordinate assistance, supplies, facilities, and labor from indigenous sources.

(8) Incorporate CMO estimates and CA assessments to develop strategy and objectives.

(9) Assess staffs and subordinate commands CA capabilities.

(10) Coordinate CAO with country teams, interagency partners, IGOs, NGOs, IPI, and HN or FN military and civilian authorities.

(11) Request guidance from the establishing authority (e.g., GCC) on implementation of multinational policies and objectives.

(12) Help allies plan and develop operational skills and infrastructure to build regional stability through CMO and CAO.

(13) Coordinate CMO and CAO planning with multinational commanders and HN forces, as directed by the establishing authority (e.g., GCC) in conjunction with the country team. Supported CCDRs and subordinate JFCs should consider establishing CMO working groups to bring all stakeholders together to focus their efforts in achieving CMO priorities.

3. Civil-Military Operations Forces and Capabilities

a. Commanders at all levels should not consider CMO the sole responsibility of SOF or specifically CA and MIS units. All US military organizations have the responsibility and capability to support CMO. CA and MIS units usually form the nucleus for CMO planning efforts; while others, such as, SOF, engineers, health services, transportation, and MP and security forces, normally function as CMO enablers. Other organizations that typically are involved in CMO, such as other government departments and agencies, IGOs, NGOs, HNs, and the private sector will be covered in Chapter IV, "Coordination."

b. **SOF**

(1) Unless otherwise directed by SecDef (assigned in Forces for Unified Commands Memorandum, found in the Global Force Management Implementation Guidance), all SOF are under the combatant command (command authority) (COCOM) of the CDRUSSOCOM. SOF are those Active Component (AC) and RC forces of the Services designated by SecDef and specifically organized, trained, and equipped to conduct and support special operations.

(2) CA and military information support operations (MISO) are mutually supportive within CMO. During some operations, MISO can be integrated with CAO activities to increase support for the HN government and reduce support to destabilizing forces. MISO can publicize the existence and successes of CAO to enhance the positive perception of US and HN actions in the operational area and transregionally. MISO inform and direct civilians concerning safety and welfare to reduce civilian casualties, suffering, and interference with military operations. Regional language and cultural expertise, and specialized communications equipment provide the capability to engage audiences with culturally accepted informative messages.

(3) **MISO** can:

(a) Gather information to assess the location, state of mind, health of local populace, and the physical characteristics of the operational area.

(b) Disseminate information to promote safety and welfare of the civilian population.

(c) Influence a civilian population's attitude toward US policy and prepare it for CMO during post conflict activities.

(d) Publicize health services and veterinary aid, construction, and public facilities activities, etc., to generate confidence in and positive perception of US and HN actions to the populace.

(e) Assist in assessments to determine the most effective application of effort and documenting the results.

(f) Support emergency relocation of DCs and for DC camp operations.

(g) As a corollary, when conducted within the framework of a viable CMO concept, CAO can contribute significantly to the overall success of MISO activities.

For further detail concerning MISO related activities and Service capabilities, refer to JP 3-13.2, Military Information Support Operations.

(4) **Civil-Military Engagement (CME)**

(a) CME is a formal United States Special Operations Command (USSOCOM) program to address specific shaping operations that support global SOF contingency plans. CME facilitates the efforts of USG departments and agencies, IGOs, NGOs, and HN to build, replace, repair, and sustain civil capabilities and capacities that eliminate, reduce, or mitigate civil vulnerabilities to local and regional populations.

(b) CME is a globally synchronized and regionally coordinated program of country-specific and regional actions executed through, and with indigenous and interagency partners, to eliminate the underlying conditions and core motivations for local and regional support to violent extremist organizations and their networks.

(c) The GCC theater special operations command (TSOC) manages and coordinates theater level CME. CME operations are coordinated with the GCC's contingency and TCPs and synchronized with the DOS mission strategic resource plan (MSRP) of the US embassy of the HN in which operations are conducted. United States Army Special Operations Command (USASOC), civil-military support elements (CMSEs) plan, execute, and assess CME.

(d) CME is designed to identify and address critical civil vulnerabilities in under-governed and ungoverned areas or high-threat environments where indigenous authorities or the country team or USAID cannot engage. In some situations, the inability to address these critical areas may be a function of HN and/or interagency lack of capacity.

(e) CME is preventive. CME supports a broader HN internal defense and development strategy by supporting the US embassy and HN government's efforts to counter violent extremism and achieve stability.

(f) CME's population-centric and indirect approach focuses on both the adversary's vulnerabilities and the vulnerabilities of the indigenous civil society. Adversary weaknesses are exploited and threats to civil society are addressed by building HN capability and capacity to eliminate the causes and drivers of instability. CME manifests itself in three lines of effort (LOEs):

1. Enable partners to combat violent extremist organizations by improving interagency and HN capacity and legitimacy; supporting key communicators and marginalizing those undermining joint efforts (also known as spoilers); and developing and fostering relationships between the HN and the CCMD, interagency, IGOs, and NGOs.

2. Deter tacit and active support of violent extremist organizations by facilitating the denial of resources, disruption, and degradation over time; and setting the conditions and support for other SOF elements to access the HN and target adversaries.

3. Erode support for extremist ideologies through pro-active and persistent engagement with the HN and interagency; and support to US and HN IO objectives.

(5) **Other SOF Support.** SOF units generally conduct CMO in operations that assist the HN or FN authorities, other government departments and agencies, NGOs, and IGOs restore peace and strengthen infrastructure. SOF are regularly employed in mobile training teams, joint and combined exercises, professional development programs, and other military-to-military activities to enhance theater security cooperation.

c. **CA**

(1) **Concept of Employment for CA**

(a) CMO staffs at every level review and update plans and orders. The CA task organization is validated by the supported GCC and included in the request for forces. The forces are sourced once the Joint Staff validates the request and assigns a force provider; USSOCOM for Army SOF-CA and United States Army Forces Command (FORSCOM) for conventional forces (CF) CA. CA forces can be tasked to deploy in support of an operational area or directly to the supported unit. The Marine Corps and Navy team provides the GCC with quick reaction capability from the sea in the form of a Marine expeditionary unit stationed aboard ships, should the need of a fast civil-military response be needed.

(b) CA assessments identify specific functional skills to support the joint force mission. These functional skills are often provided through reach back to US based CA functional specialists.

(c) The US Army civil affairs commands (CACOMs) provide CA capability to five geographic CCMDs: US Pacific Command, US European Command, US Central Command, US Africa Command, and US Southern Command. CACOMs align with the

GCCs; however, one CACOM supports both US European Command and US Africa Command. CACOMs develop plans, policy, and programs through planning teams, fusion of CIM, regional engagement, and civil component analysis at the strategic and theater level.

(d) Requests for mobilization are initiated through the Joint Staff and DOD. When authorized, reserve CA elements are mobilized and deployed. A majority of CA forces are located in the Army Reserve.

(2) **CAO.** CA forces are a force multiplier for JFCs. CA functions are conducted by CA teams, to include civil affairs teams (CATs) at tactical levels, civil affairs planning teams (CAPTs), and civil liaison teams (CLTs) at tactical and operational levels; CMSEs at operational and theater strategic levels; and CMOCs with functional specialty and CIM capabilities at all levels. Individual members can augment joint force headquarters, while units can be attached to or support joint force components.

(a) Tactical level CATs are designed to provide the maneuver commander direct interaction with the civilian population.

(b) CA units form the nucleus of the CMOC to:

<u>1.</u> Facilitate collaborative civil-military efforts with other USG departments and agencies, NGOs, IGOs, and IPI.

<u>2.</u> Provide direct functional specialist support to HN or FN ministries (US Army).

<u>3.</u> Provide the supported commander a CIM coordinator to consolidate civil information, conduct content management, and coordinate civil data sharing.

(c) CA units augment the joint force CMO staff element or subordinate commands' staff to provide specialized CA skills.

For more information see Chapter IV, "Civil Affairs Forces and Civil Affairs Operations."

(3) **Policies.** CAO always comply with international and domestic law, but will vary with US foreign policy, the military situation, the presence of MNFs, and other factors. Commanders should request guidance from appropriate authorities in ambiguous situations.

(a) **Policy Flow.** CAO is guided by policy developed by the President or SecDef and are transmitted to commanders through command channels.

(b) **US Commanders Serving as MNF Commanders.** MNF policies are normally developed by agreement between member nations and provided to commanders through a council of ministers or a similar policy making body. Should multinational CMO guidance be in conflict with US law, international law, or specific national instructions, commanders must immediately request guidance through US channels. MNF commanders operating as part of a North Atlantic Treaty Organization (NATO) force or with NATO forces should be mindful of the principles of civil-military cooperation (CIMIC), which govern CMO for NATO forces (to include US forces under such circumstances). See subparagraph 4i for additional CIMIC details.

(c) **GCCs**. Policies concerning the scope of CMO and procedural guidance normally are covered in an Executive Order or by a policy directive originating within the NSC. Commanders receive guidance transmitted through SecDef and the CJCS. Commanders provide guidance to subordinate commanders, including specific instructions regarding the exercise of authority for CAO. Commanders should liaise with supporting CCDRs to work with US diplomatic representatives in their own AORs to coordinate CAO.

d. **Intelligence.** The operational relationship between intelligence and CMO is mutually enhancing, yet highly sensitive. In complex OEs, cultural or situational awareness and understanding and other information of potential intelligence value may originate from open sources derived from personal contacts and relationships through diplomacy, commercial activities, and CMO activities. Key leader engagement, CIM, and CMOC activities can enhance the commander's situational awareness. CA personnel acquire a variety of information, but they must not violate intelligence gathering restrictions. Intelligence personnel operating openly and directly with CA can jeopardize CA personnel and the CMO mission. JFCs should delineate responsibility between CMO and intelligence with robust, yet discreet, operational lines of coordination to manage risks. Defense support to public diplomacy coordinates the JFC's CMO themes with other USG departments and agencies. DOS leads public diplomacy with DOD in a supporting role. All communications must be in concert with strategic guidance.

e. **Engineering**

(1) Engineer operations support the local civilian population through such projects as building roads and public facilities. They also coordinate engineer assets from nonmilitary organizations and military forces. Engineer operations typically include DOD civilians, NGOs, IGOs, interagency partners, and contractors.

(2) **Capabilities**. Engineer units support the JFC through combat engineering, geospatial engineering, and general engineering (GE). US military engineer units provide specialized capabilities as depicted in Figure II-1. Technical engineering support and contract support are provided by a variety of supporting organizations. The HN may also have engineering capabilities specifically adapted to the local environment. Contractors and multinational military engineers in an immature theater also can provide valuable capabilities. Engineer requirements will change throughout the operation so the JFC should manage engineer capabilities across Service lines.

(3) **Support to CMO.** Within a joint force, engineers may operate with other government departments and agencies, NGOs, IGOs, and the private sector. Establishing and maintaining effective liaison with all participating agencies is critical to achieving unity of effort. The CMOC, especially the organic CIM capability, can be a focal point within the joint force for coordination with these agencies and organizations.

Specialized Engineering Capabilities

- Firefighting services
- Well-drilling
- Underwater construction
- Construction and repair of airfields and ports to include associated support equipment
- Maintenance of lines of communications
- Explosive hazard neutralization
- Environmental assessments
- Erection of bare base facilities
- Construction of fuels and water supply
- Power generation
- Facilities engineering and management
- Real estate management
- Waste disposal
- Public utilities, reconstruction/revitalization projects
- Force protection enhancement

Figure II-1. Specialized Engineering Capabilities

For further detail concerning Service capabilities and other related engineer activities, refer to Appendix A, "Service Capabilities," and JP 3-34, Joint Engineer Operations.

f. **Health Services**

(1) The use of health services has historically proven to be a valuable low-risk asset in support of CMO. Health services are generally a noncontroversial and cost-effective means of using the military to support US national interests in another country. Health service initiatives should be primarily focused on preventive programs and capacity-building activities that are sustainable by the HN. Health service operations conducted to enhance the stability of an HN should be well coordinated with all concerned agencies, including USAID, NGOs, and integrated into the respective US embassy plans. Independent, unplanned, health-service civic-action programs should not be undertaken. If any direct patient care activities are undertaken, issues of credentialing, liability, standards of care, and patient hand-off need to be addressed prior to engagement.

For more details, refer to JP 4-02, Health Services.

(2) **Health Support Activities.** Health support activities in support of CMO include medical services, dental treatment, veterinarian and preventive medicine services, medical logistics, and aeromedical evacuation. CMO planners should take into consideration

the legal and policy issues regarding the treatment of foreign civilians and a greater focus on the prevention and treatment of diseases.

(3) **Policies.** The joint force surgeon is responsible for health support policies and procedures based on the commander's estimate of the situation. Medical intelligence provides JFCs occupational and environmental threat analysis to improve force health protection (FHP). Where practical, dual use of available health support assets should be considered to support CMO requirements and military operations.

(4) **Support to CMO**

(a) Health support activities in CMO are illustrated in Figure II-2. Additional health support activities are listed in JP 4-02, *Health Services*.

(b) Health support activities support and enhance the HN health sector infrastructure by:

1. Developing medical programs tailored for the HN (e.g., appropriate and affordable).

2. Developing sustainable training and acquisition programs.

3. Increasing the effectiveness of other USG department and agency programs such as USAID and DOS public diplomacy.

Health Support Activities in Civil-Military Operations

- Public health activities, to include preventive medicine and veterinary care, food sanitation, water quality monitoring, sanitary facility evaluations, immunizations of humans and animals, pediatric medical support, and resuscitation and stabilization of acute illness and injuries
- Diagnostic and treatment training
- Development of health support logistic programs
- Development of continuing health support education programs
- Development of medical intelligence and threat analysis
- Development of a host nation military field health support system for treatment and evacuation
- Assistance in the upgrade, staffing, and supplying logistic support of existing health support facilities
- Disease vector control/surveillance operations
- Medical stability operations and building partner capacity for biosecurity and humanitarian assistance/disaster response

Figure II-2. Health Support Activities in Civil-Military Operations

---

<u>4</u>. Recommending and coordinating health services education opportunities for HN personnel.

<u>5</u>. Coordination with NGOs for long-term sustainability.

(c) Improving the economic well-being through veterinary medicine and animal husbandry.

For further detail concerning Service capabilities, refer to Appendix A, "Service Capabilities."

g. **Transportation**

(1) JFCs may use a variety of military and commercial transportation resources, to include airlift, sealift, land surface transportation, overseas resources (including vehicles), port operations, pre-positioning programs, and intermodal resources. The Commander, United States Transportation Command (CDRUSTRANSCOM) provides common-user air, land, and sea transportation for DOD. Except for Service-organic or theater-assigned assets, or HN transportation support assets the GCC has negotiated, CDRUSTRANSCOM exercises COCOM of the strategic transportation assets of the Military Departments and is the DOD single manager for transportation. CDRUSTRANSCOM aligns traffic management and transportation single manager responsibilities. GCCs assigned transportation assets should ensure they are interoperable with the Defense Transportation System. GCCs secure transportation assets at forward locations through subordinate commanders.

For further information on transportation operations, refer to JP 4-01, The Defense Transportation System.

(2) **Transportation Activities** Transportation organizations plan, coordinate, conduct, monitor, and control intertheater and intratheater movement of personnel and materiel.

EQUIPMENT REQUIREMENTS IN CIVIL-MILITARY OPERATIONS

In the aftermath of Hurricane MITCH, the devastated nations of Central America requested helicopter support to distribute relief supplies as well as conduct search and rescue operations in areas that had been cut off by land slides, road washouts, and bridge damage. As USSOUTHCOM [US Southern Command] planners executed Operation FUERTES APOYO, a strictly civil-military operation; helicopter units were the first to deploy, and were followed by engineer and bridging units. The ability of helicopters to access remote areas was critical during the response phase of the operation, when the priority of effort was to save lives. Later, during rehabilitation and restoration phases, as roads were cleared and bridges repaired, helicopters redeployed as less expensive ground transportation could again be utilized.

Source: United States Southern Command—Hurricane MITCH 1998

---

(3) **Assets.** JFCs conducting CMO can use assigned components' transportation assets as well as United States Transportation Command support. Organic transportation varies with force composition but typically will include trucks, helicopters, and possibly watercraft. A versatile mix of these assets is normally organic to deployed Navy amphibious warfare ships.

(4) **Support to CMO.** Military transportation organizations can distribute food, water, and medical supplies; conduct health services evacuation; and move DCs to a safe environment. Some of these organizations can help restore HN civilian transportation infrastructure. The versatility of military transportation assets (air, sea, and land) allows the JFC to select the mode of transportation most appropriate for the situation. JFCs should also evaluate the feasibility of using other transportation system infrastructure. This will enable a smooth transition to civil stability operations and ensure a source of revenue when establishing a new national government. Services have robust air traffic control capabilities and are certified to Federal Aviation Administration standards. However, these capabilities do not directly translate to international air traffic control within military channels, therefore detailed plans should address what civil agencies or contract organizations will eventually act as the interim service provider and transition agency from military to civil control.

For further detail concerning Service transportation assets and capabilities, refer to Appendix A, "Service Capabilities."

h. **MP or Security Forces**

(1) MP or security forces are trained to exercise authority in tense circumstances without escalating tension. MP or security forces can sometimes defuse tension because of their law-enforcement training. They can also train other supporting forces such as engineers, and special operations to use nonlethal capabilities within the use of force continuum.

(2) **MP or Security Forces Activities.** MP or security forces activities are shown in Figure II-3.

(3) **Policies.** Commanders should understand the legal basis for MP or security forces and law enforcement (LE) activities in FN. Policies must be in place with regards to collection and sharing of identity information of HN and/or other personnel. They must also provide appropriate direction to subordinate commanders.

(4) **Assets.** The Services have a variety of MP or security forces organizations to provide the joint force significant capabilities.

(5) **Support to CMO.** MP or security forces are well suited for CMO. MP or security forces can staff checkpoints, liaise with HN police forces, and conduct or assist with traffic control, DC operations, and FP operations.

(a) Commanders should consult with the ambassador, joint force staff judge advocate (SJA), provost marshal, CA representatives interagency partners, HN, FN, IGO, and NGO representatives to mitigate HN hostility against MP or security forces activities.

Military Police or Security Forces Activities

- Convoy defense
- Patrolling and manning checkpoints
- Reaction force
- Liaison to civilian police forces
- Investigations of criminal activity
- Handling, processing, safeguarding, and accounting for hostile individuals
- Physical security and preservation of order
- Dislocated civilian processing
- Populace and resource control
- Force protection
- Traffic control

Figure II-3. Military Police or Security Forces Activities

(b) Training and support of foreign police forces is tightly governed by US law and policy. Commanders should understand US law and policy related to training or establishing FN police forces.

For further detail on Service MP or security forces capabilities, refer to Appendix A, "Service Capabilities."

4. Organizing for Civil-Military Operations

a. **J-9 CMO Directorate.** CMO are often key enablers to successful joint operations. J-9 builds relations with military and civilian organizations that influence operations or campaigns. The J-9 coordinates with a variety of organizations that have their own agendas and objectives to enable collaborative planning. The J-9 provides a conduit for information sharing, coordinating support requests and activities, compiling and analyzing relevant information, and performing analysis that supports the commander's assessment. J-9 staff functions may include:

(1) Serve as staff proponent for the organization, use, and integration of attached CA forces.

(2) Provide liaison as needed to interagency partners, NGOs, IGOs, and other joint task forces (JTFs).

(3) Provide staff oversight and direction to the CMOC if established by the JFC.

(4) Develop annex G (Civil Affairs) and assist in the development of annex V (Interagency Coordination) to operation plans and operation orders.

(5) Coordinate with the comptroller and SJA to obtain advise on proposed expenditures of allocated funds, dedicated to CMO. Facilitate movement, security, and control of funds to subordinate units; and coordinate with the funds controlling authority and financial manager to meet the commander's objectives.

(6) Support transition operations (terminated, transferred to follow-on forces, or transitioned to USG departments and agencies, IPI, or IGOs) as required.

(7) Provide expertise and support to the joint interagency coordination group (JIACG) or joint interagency task force if either is part of the joint staff.

(8) Organize a CIM coordination capability to manage execution of the joint-CIM process in the supported commanders' operational area.

For further details on joint staff directorates, see JP 3-33, Joint Task Force Headquarters.

b. **JTF**

(1) JTFs may conduct CMO during any military operation.

(2) SecDef, a GCC, a subunified commander, or an existing JTF commander may establish a joint civil-military operations task force (JCMOTF), joint military information support task force (JMISTF), or joint special operations task force (JSOTF) when the size and scope of CMO, MISO, or special operations in the JOA requires coordination and activities which exceeds current staff capacity.

(3) Figure II-4 illustrates possible JTF organization.

For further JTF guidance, refer to JP 1, Doctrine for the Armed Forces of the United States, *and JP 3-33,* Joint Task Force Headquarters.

c. **JCMOTF.** JFCs may establish a JCMOTF when the scope of CMO requirements and activities are beyond the JFC's organic capability.

(1) JCMOTFs are configured for specific CMO requirements such as stability operations. Figure II-5 highlights some of the typical JCMOTF functions.

(a) The composition of this organization should be representative of the forces comprising the JCMOTF. A JCMOTF may have both CF and SOF assigned or attached. United States Army CA commands and brigades or the maritime civil affairs and security training (MCAST) Command organizational structure can provide the operational C2 structure to form a JCMOTF. A notional JCMOTF staff organization is depicted in Figure II-6.

(b) A JCMOTF is a US joint force organization, similar in organization to a JSOTF or JTF, and is flexible in size and composition. It usually is subordinate to a JTF, or it can function as a stand-alone organization.

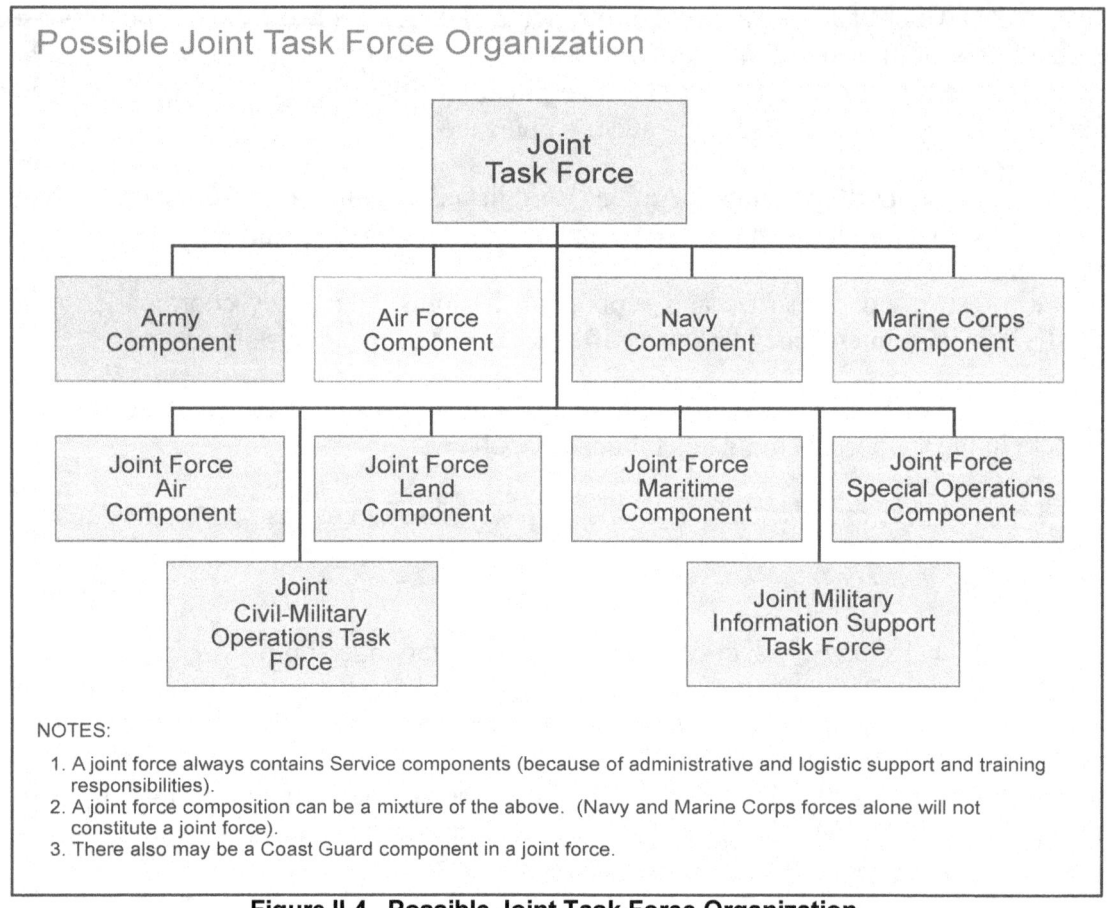

Figure II-4. **Possible Joint Task Force Organization**

(c) A JCMOTF can be formed in theater, in the US (within the limits of the law), or in both locations, depending on scope, duration, or sensitivity of the CMO requirement and associated policy considerations.

(2) JCMOTFs can:

(a) Consolidate and coordinate CMO.

(b) Provide unity of command.

(c) Allow the JFC to centralize CMO and transition efforts under one headquarters.

d. **JMISTF.** A JMISTF is appropriate when the requested MIS force size and planned disposition may exceed the C2 capabilities of the joint force components. The JFC may establish a JMISTF or military information support task force (MISTF) as a component of the joint force. The CCDR may establish the JMISTF or MISTF as a component of an existing joint force component such as a JSOTF or special operations task force. MIS forces may be organized as large as a JMISTF or as small as a MIS team that provides a planning capability. A JMISTF gives the JFC flexibility to arrange the C2 structure of attached or assigned MIS forces.

> ## Typical Functions Performed by a Joint Civil-Military Operations Task Force
>
> - Advise the commander, joint task force (CJTF), on policy; funding; multinational, foreign, or host nation sensitivities; and their effect on theater strategy and/or campaign and operational missions.
>
> - Provide command and control or direction of military host nation advisory, assessment, planning, and other assistance activities by joint US forces.
>
> - Assist in establishing US or multinational and military-to-civil links for greater efficiency of cooperative assistance arrangements.
>
> - Perform essential coordination or liaison with host nation agencies, country team, United Nations agencies, and deployed US multinational, host-nation military forces, and supporting logistic organizations.
>
> - Assist in the planning and conduct of civil information programs to publicize positive results and objectives of military assistance projects, to build civil acceptance and support of US operations, and to promote indigenous capabilities contributing to recovery and economic-social development.
>
> - Plan and conduct joint and combined civil-military operations training exercises.
>
> - Advise and assist in strengthening or stabilizing civil infrastructures and services and otherwise facilitating transition to peacekeeping or consolidation operations and associated hand-off to other government agencies, intergovernmental organizations, or host nation responsibility.
>
> - Assess or identify host-nation civil support, relief, or funding requirements to the CJTF for transmission to supporting commanders, Services, or other responsible United States Government departments or agencies.

Figure II-5. Typical Functions Performed by a Joint Civil-Military Operations Task Force

For further details on JMISTFs, refer to JP 3-13.2, Military Information Support Operations.

e. **Humanitarian Operations Center (HOC).** The HOC is a senior level international and interagency coordinating body designed to achieve unity of effort in a large FHA operation. HOCs are horizontally structured with no C2 authority. All members are responsible to their own organizations or countries. The HOC normally is established under the direction of the government of the affected country or the UN, or possibly the USAID Office of United States Foreign Disaster Assistance (OFDA) during a US unilateral operation. Because the HOC operates at the national level, it should consist of senior representatives from the affected country, the US embassy, joint force, OFDA, NGOs, IGOs, and other major organizations in the operation.

f. **Humanitarian Assistance Coordination Center (HACC).** During FHA operations, CCDRs may organize a HACC to assist with interagency partners, IGO, and NGO coordination and planning. Normally, the HACC is a temporary body that operates in early planning and coordination stages. Once a CMOC or HOC is established, the role of the HACC diminishes, and its functions are accomplished through normal CCDR's staff and crisis action organization.

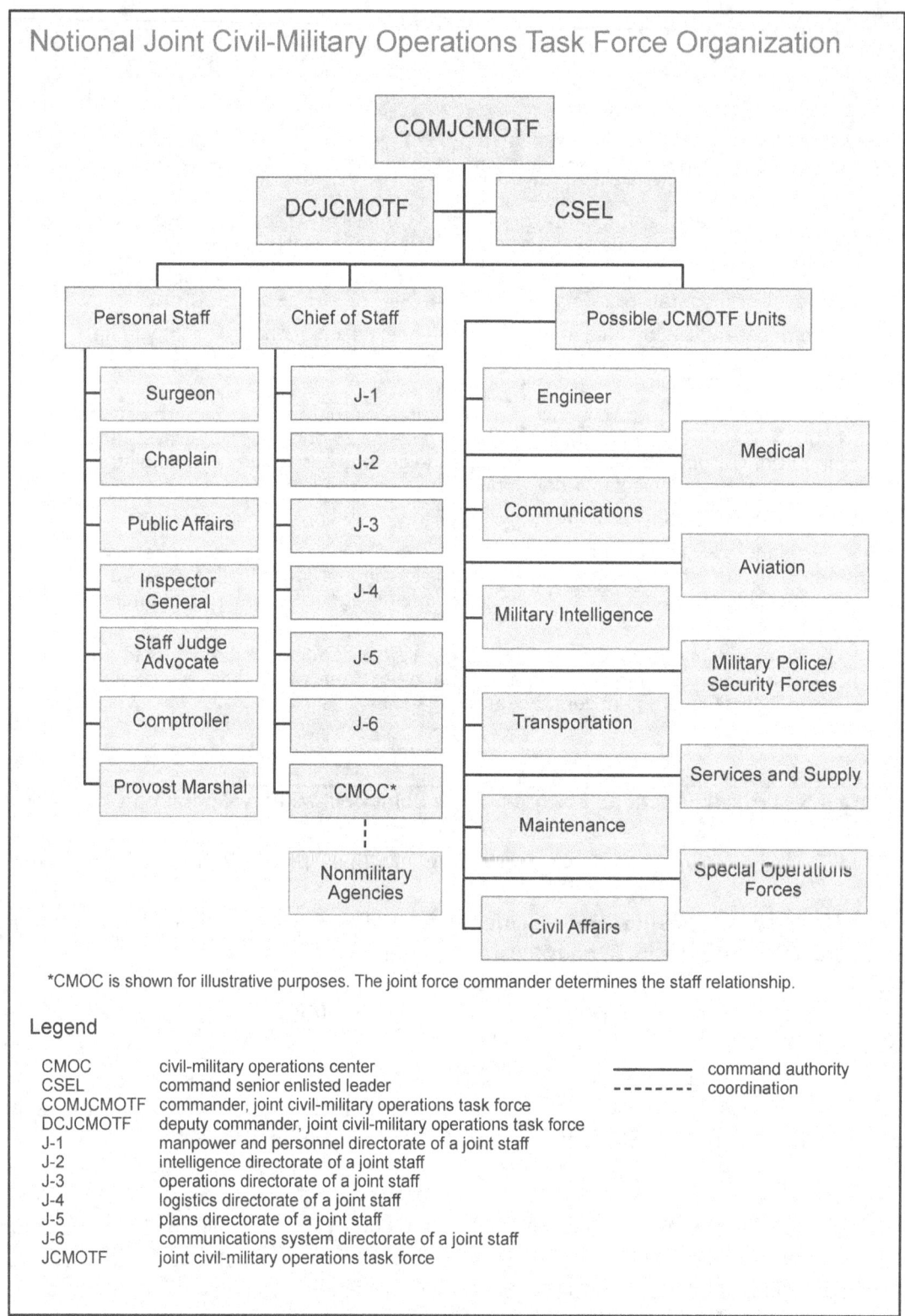

Notional Joint Civil-Military Operations Task Force Organization

COMJCMOTF

DCJCMOTF — CSEL

Personal Staff | Chief of Staff | Possible JCMOTF Units

Personal Staff
- Surgeon
- Chaplain
- Public Affairs
- Inspector General
- Staff Judge Advocate
- Comptroller
- Provost Marshal

Chief of Staff
- J-1
- J-2
- J-3
- J-4
- J-5
- J-6
- CMOC*
  - Nonmilitary Agencies

Possible JCMOTF Units
- Engineer
- Medical
- Communications
- Aviation
- Military Intelligence
- Military Police/ Security Forces
- Transportation
- Services and Supply
- Maintenance
- Special Operations Forces
- Civil Affairs

*CMOC is shown for illustrative purposes. The joint force commander determines the staff relationship.

Legend

CMOC	civil-military operations center	———	command authority
CSEL	command senior enlisted leader	--------	coordination
COMJCMOTF	commander, joint civil-military operations task force		
DCJCMOTF	deputy commander, joint civil-military operations task force		
J-1	manpower and personnel directorate of a joint staff		
J-2	intelligence directorate of a joint staff		
J-3	operations directorate of a joint staff		
J-4	logistics directorate of a joint staff		
J-5	plans directorate of a joint staff		
J-6	communications system directorate of a joint staff		
JCMOTF	joint civil-military operations task force		

Figure II-6. Notional Joint Civil-Military Operations Task Force Organization

JOINT TASK FORCE-HAITI HUMANITARIAN ASSISTANCE COORDINATION CENTER

The joint task force (JTF)-Haiti commander organized boards, centers, cells, and working groups to facilitate collaboration and align JTF operations with the United Nations (UN) Stabilization Mission in Haiti and other partners. JTF-Haiti stood up a 30-person humanitarian assistance coordination cell (HACC) as a civil-military operations center like mechanism to integrate with the UN cluster system. The JTF Commander designated Brigadier General Matern, a Canadian exchange officer assigned to the XVIII Airborne Corps Headquarters, the responsibility to lead the HACC efforts. Primarily staffed by members of the 96th Civil Affairs Battalion, the HACC began the task of integrating US military support to the United States Agency for International Development (USAID), the UN cluster system, and the Government of Haiti by coordinating, planning, and assisting the establishment of medical clinics and food and water distribution points. The JTF also provided key support to the staffs and working groups of USAID and the UN. Possibly the most important assistance provided was in the area of planning and planners. A UN strategic plans officer recently commented about Operation UNIFIED RESPONSE. The military's planning capability is not the most expensive part, but it is probably the most valuable. The international coordination structure would not have stood up as quickly if they were not tapped into the JTF planning capacity.

Various Sources

g. **CMOC**

(1) CMOCs are tailored to the mission and augmented by engineer, medical, and transportation assets to the supported commander. The CMOC is the primary coordination interface for US forces and IPI, humanitarian organizations, IGOs, NGOs, MNFs, HN government agencies, and other USG departments and agencies. The CMOC facilitates coordination among the key participants.

(2) A CMOC is formed to:

(a) Execute JFC CMO guidance.

(b) Lead JFC CIM.

(c) Liaise with other departments, agencies, and organizations.

(d) Provide a joint force forum for organizations which want to maintain their neutrality. Many of these organizations consider the CMOC as a venue for stakeholder discussions, but not a stakeholder decision-making forum.

(e) Receive, validate, and coordinate requests for support from NGOs, IGOs, and the private sector. The CMOC then forwards these requests to the joint force for action.

(3) CMOC-type organizations should be convenient for interorganizational partners and use joint force communications, transportation, and staff planning capacity to develop unity of effort. JFC should build the CMOC from organic assets and CA personnel, logistic, legal, and communications elements. United States Army (USA) CA units are organized to provide the JFC the manpower and equipment to form the nucleus of the CMOC. CMOCs generally have representatives from:

(a) Liaisons from Service and functional components.

(b) USAID representatives.

(c) Embassy country team and other USG representatives.

(d) Military liaison personnel from participating countries.

(e) Host country or local government agency representatives.

(f) Representatives of NGOs, IGOs, and the private sector (as appropriate).

(4) The composition of a notional CMOC is illustrated in Figure II-7. It is not the intent of this figure to emphasize the CMOC as the center of coordination for all activities,

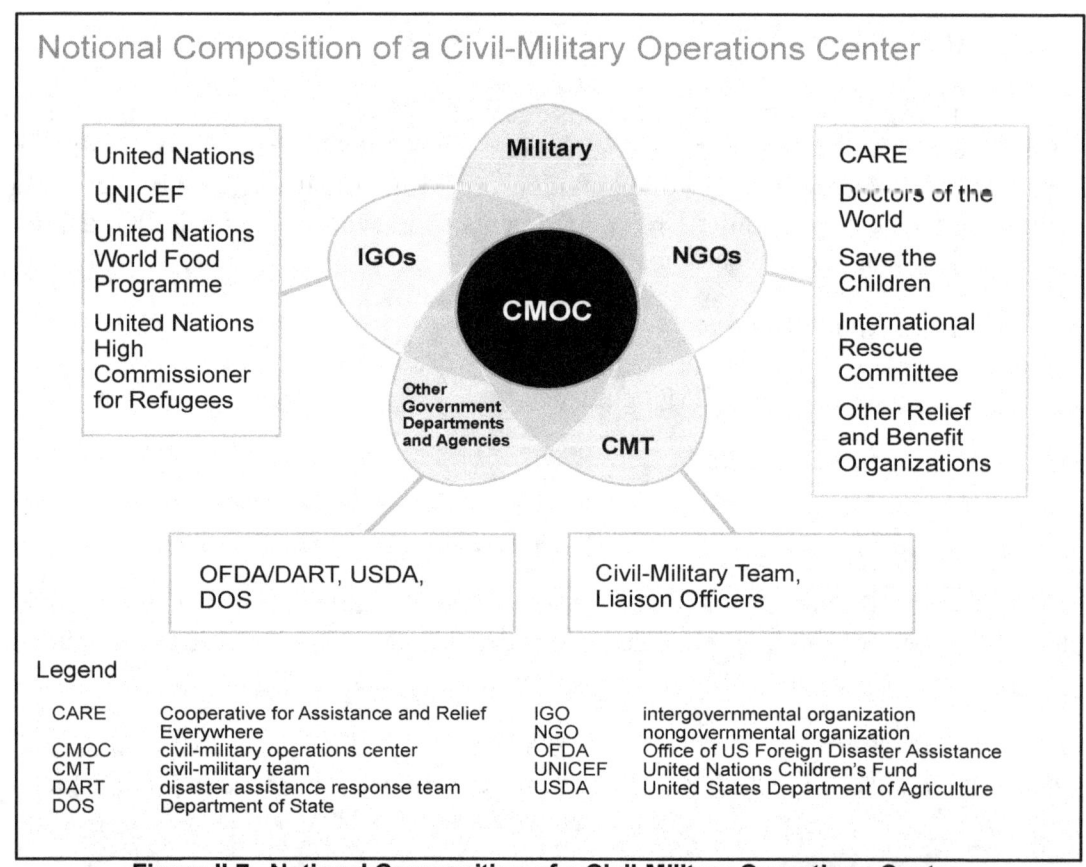

Figure II-7. Notional Composition of a Civil-Military Operations Center

but rather to illustrate organizations that a JFC may cooperate with and hold discussions with concerning an ongoing operation.

(5) Political representatives in the CMOC may provide avenues to coordinate military and political actions. The CMOC may provide NGOs and IGOs a single point of coordination with US forces and help promote unified action.

(a) It is incumbent on the military not to attempt to dictate what will happen but to coordinate a unified approach to problem resolution.

(b) A JFC cannot direct interagency cooperation. The CMOC can help identify security, logistic support, information sharing, communications, and other issues that require collaboration.

(6) Figure II-8 depicts some of the CMOC functions.

(7) A joint force public affairs officer (PAO) or PA representative and IO representative should attend recurring CMOC meetings as the PAO is the only official spokesperson for the JFC other than the JFC himself. As active members of the CMOC,

---

Civil-Military Operations Center Functions

- Provide nonmilitary agencies with a focal point for activities and matters that are civilian related.
- Coordinate relief efforts with US or multinational commands, United Nations, host nation, and other nonmilitary agencies.
- Assist in the transfer of humanitarian responsibility to nonmilitary agencies.
- Facilitate and coordinate activities of the joint force, other on-scene agencies, and higher echelons in the military chain of command.
- Receive, validate, coordinate, and monitor requests from humanitarian organizations for routine and emergency military support.
- Coordinate the response to requests for military support with Service components.
- Coordinate requests to nonmilitary agencies for their support.
- Coordinate with the disaster assistance response team deployed by the US Agency for International Development/Office of US Foreign Disaster Assistance.
- Convene ad hoc mission planning groups to address complex military missions that support nonmilitary requirements, such as convoy escort, and management and security of dislocated civilian camps and feeding centers.
- Convene follow-on assessment groups.

Figure II-8. Civil-Military Operations Center Functions

those PA and IO representatives work with other CMOC representatives (as available) to help develop themes, messages, and specific news stories that adhere to strategic guidance. Additionally, a senior CMOC representative should attend the CCMD/JTF battle rhythm events that discuss IO and the commander's communication synchronization issues.

(8) The CMOC officer in charge (OIC) typically reports to the CMO officer on the staff. The OIC might be assigned to the J-9, the chief of staff (COS), or the commander of the JCMOTF if established. During certain operations, such as the conduct of FHA, the JFC might assign a deputy commander or the COS as the director of the CMOC perhaps with another officer assigned to provide detailed supervision of its operation. The CMOC officer requires access to the JFC based on the situation and mission.

(9) The USG may establish a crisis reaction center (CRC) as part of a response package prior to the arrival of a JTF. CMOC personnel may integrate with the established USG CRC to mitigate duplication of effort. USG departments and agencies, IPI, IGOs, NGOs, and MNFs coordinating with an established CRC may not interface with a CMOC. However, the JTF should be prepared to create a CMOC in the event the CRC is overwhelmed by the situation, or in another location based on the JTF's mission. See Figure II-9 for a comparison between a HOC, HACC, and CMOC.

h. **Civil-Military Teams.** A civil-military team helps stabilize the OE in a province, district, state, or locality through its combined diplomatic, informational, military, and economic capabilities. It combines representatives from interagency (and perhaps multinational) partners into a cohesive unit capable of independently conducting operations to stabilize a part of the OE by enhancing the legitimacy and the effectiveness of the HN government. A civil-military team can focus on combined military and civil efforts to diminish the means and motivations of conflict, while developing local institutions so they can take the lead role in national governance, providing basic services, economic development, and enforcing the rule of law. Examples of civil-military teaming include the provincial reconstruction teams (PRTs) which were used in Operations IRAQI FREEDOM and NEW DAWN in Iraq, and Operation ENDURING FREEDOM in Afghanistan.

(1) PRTs are designed to stabilize and enable civil authority. Joint force planners and interorganizational partners should organize and train the PRT early in the JOPP. As progress is made in stabilizing the area, the PRT will transition to civil authorities.

(2) PRTs focus on the provincial government and local infrastructure. Normally, PRTs are assigned by province but may be assigned to local governments within a province, or to more than one province.

(3) PRT functions may include:

(a) Provide international military presence to help develop nascent HN security and rule of law capacity.

(b) Advise and empower stakeholders and local government officials to establish and improve legitimate government bodies.

Comparison Between Humanitarian Operations Center, Humanitarian Assistance Coordination Center, and Civil-Military Operations Center

	Establishing Authority	Function	Composition
Humanitarian Operations Center (HOC)	Designated individual of affected country, United Nations (UN), or United States Government (USG) department or agency	Coordinates overall relief strategy at the national (country) level.	Representatives from: • affected country • UN • US embassy or consulate • joint task force • other nonmilitary agencies • concerned parties (private sector)
Humanitarian Assistance Coordination Center	Combatant commander	Assists with interagency coordination and planning at the strategic level. Normally is disestablished once a HOC or CMOC is established.	Representatives from: • combatant command • nongovernmental organizations • intergovernmental organizations • regional organizations • concerned parties (private sector)
Civil-Military Operations Center (CMOC)	Joint task force or component commander	Assists in coordination of activities at the operational level and tactical level with military forces, USG departments and agencies, nongovernmental and intergovernmental organizations, and regional organizations.	Representatives from: • joint task force • nongovernmental organizations • intergovernmental organizations • regional organizations • USG departments and agencies • local government (host country) • multinational forces • other concerned parties (private sector)

The authority of all three centers is coordination only.

Figure II-9. Comparison Between Humanitarian Operations Center, Humanitarian Assistance Coordination Center, and Civil-Military Operations Center

(c) Plan reconstruction with interorganizational partners to provide basic services, build a functional economy, promote representative government, and decrease reliance on international assistance.

(4) Military participation in the PRT will vary with operational requirements, but should include CA personnel and security and staff support as required. Interagency memoranda of agreement which define roles, responsibilities, and funding are required to establish PRTs. PRT members should train as a unit to facilitate unity of effort.

i. **NATO CIMIC.** Allied doctrine uses CIMIC to describe CMO. CIMIC staff elements for the NATO commander provide essentially the same functions as CMO staff elements for the JFC. Similar to a CMOC, NATO commanders may establish CIMIC centers at operational and tactical levels solely to communicate and coordinate with interorganizational partners.

For further details concerning CIMIC, refer to Allied Joint Publication (AJP) 3.4.9, Allied Joint Doctrine for Civil-Military Cooperation.

CIVIL-MILITARY TEAM

The first several hours after a major natural disaster such as the Haiti earthquake constitute a period of "incomplete situational awareness." During this time, the situation is changing rapidly, communications are disrupted, access is limited, and most on-the-ground assessments have not yet been conducted. Because of its proximity to Haiti, the US was quickly able to dispatch a USAID [United States Agency for International Development] disaster assistance response team (DART) and USSOUTHCOM [United States Southern Command] personnel set up US Joint Task Force Haiti to manage and coordinate logistics and to support other USG [United States Government] humanitarian response activities. Coordination centers were established at USSOUTHCOM in Miami and at USAID and State Department [Department of State] in Washington to gather information that was useful for strategic and programmatic decision making. One lesson learned/best practice that was followed was the assigning of DOD [Department of Defense], DOS [Department of State], and USAID personnel in each other's coordination centers to serve as liaisons and advisors in an effort to develop and implement a "whole-of-government" approach to the response. Representatives from UN [United Nations] agencies and NGOs [nongovernmental organizations] also served as liaisons in some of these coordination centers, as well as with some USG teams in Haiti. This helped to establish personal relationships, facilitate interorganizational information sharing, and provide greater understanding of cross-community cultures.

US Department of State
Humanitarian Information Unit
White Paper July 2010

j. **UN Operations**

(1) **United Nations Humanitarian Civil-Military Coordination (UN CMCoord).** The UN CMCoord Officer Field Handbook describes military support to UN operations as, "The essential dialogue and interaction between civilian and military actors in humanitarian emergencies that is necessary to protect and promote humanitarian principles, avoid competition, minimize inconsistency, and when appropriate pursue common goals." The key elements of UN CMCoord are information sharing, task division, and planning. Basic strategies range from coexistence to cooperation. Coordination is a shared responsibility facilitated by liaison and common training. The humanitarian and military actors have fundamentally different institutional thinking and cultures, characterized by the distinct chain-of-command and clear organizational structures of the military vis-à-vis the diversity of the humanitarian community. Civil-military coordination is a shared responsibility of the humanitarian and military actors.

(2) Coordination with the UN begins at the national level with the DOS through the US Representative to the UN. The US Representative to the UN may be an invited member of the NSC and participates in the formulation of policy matters relevant to the UN and its activities. An assistant from one of the Services coordinates appropriate military interest

---

During Operation ENDURING FREEDOM (OEF) and Operation IRAQI FREEDOM (OIF), coalition forces established provincial reconstruction teams (PRTs) throughout Afghanistan and Iraq. Although PRTs were used in both operations to help stabilize the operational environment following major combat operations, the structure, oversight, and implementation differed in several significant ways.

OEF PRTs

All US-led PRTs commanded by military officer. PRTs generally maintain their own forward operating bases with their own force protection and support services. More focus on helping local governments rebuild infrastructure to meet basic needs.

Each PRT has a different structure that meets the needs of the individual area of operations. Coalition PRTs are structured differently than US PRTs, and each coalition PRT reflects that countries unique organizational structures and philosophies.

OIF PRTs

PRTs led by senior Foreign Service officer.

PRTs generally collocated with combat forces on an established base where support services are provided. Less focus on rebuilding infrastructure, more focus on coaching and mentoring government officials to build and grow the economies of their provinces. PRTs generally share a modular organizational structure.

Source: **Provincial Reconstruction Teams in Iraq:**
Tactics, Techniques, and Procedures
Center for Army Lessons Learned
January 2007

primarily with the United Nation's Office for the Coordination of Humanitarian Affairs (UNOCHA) and the United Nations Department for Peacekeeping Operations (UNDPKO).

(3) The Foreign Assistance Act of 1961, The United Nations Participation Act of 1945, and Executive Order 10206, Providing for Support of United Nations' Activities Directed to the Peaceful Settlements of Disputes, authorize various types of US military support to the UN.

(4) US military operations in support of the UN usually fall within Chapter VI, *"Pacific Settlement of Disputes,"* or Chapter VII, *"Action with Respect to Threats to the Peace, Breaches of the Peace, and Acts of Aggression,"* of the UN Charter.

(5) The UN normally conducts PO or FHA under the provisions of a resolution or mandate from the Security Council or the General Assembly. Politicians and diplomats trying to reach compromise develop mandates. The political and diplomatic nature of UN mandates often make them difficult to translate into workable mission orders.

Commanders can use the interagency process and the USG strategic plan for reconstruction, stabilization, or conflict transformation (if developed) to feed back their concerns through the political apparatus of the UN. The JFC should always seek to clarify the mission with the ambassador or UN resident coordinator, as appropriate.

(6) The UN headquarters coordinate PO and FHA around the world. The UN organizes with headquarters and the operational field elements. UN headquarters are a combined strategic and operational level, and field elements are separate tactical-level equivalent to deployed elements of the Armed Forces of the United States.

(7) At the headquarters, the Secretariat plans and directs missions. Either the UNDPKO or the UNOCHA serves as the headquarters component during emergencies. The Joint Staff and service headquarters may provide additional support by temporary augmentation for specific requirements.

(8) Field-level organization often is based on the resident coordinator system administered by the UN Development Program in conjunction with the UNOCHA. The resident coordinator mobilizes and manages the local UN humanitarian resources and provides direction for the field relief effort.

(9) In certain emergencies, the UN Secretary General (SYG) may appoint a special representative who reports to the SYG directly, as well as advises UNDPKO and UNOCHA at UN headquarters. The special representative may direct day-to-day operations.

(10) JFCs may need a direct channel to either the resident coordinator, the special representative of the SYG, or both. The joint force deployment order should establish arrangements between the joint force and UN forces.

(11) UN-sponsored operations normally employ a force under a single commander. The force commander is appointed by the SYG with the consent of the UN Security Council and reports directly to the SYG's special representative or to the SYG. In any multinational operation, the US commander will retain command authority over all assigned US forces. The US chain of command will flow from SecDef through the GCC. On a case-by-case basis, the President may consider placing appropriate US forces under the operational control of a UN commander for specific UN operations authorized by the Security Council.

k. **Other Organizational Humanitarian Structures.** In an affected country or joint operational area there may be other humanitarian relief organizations with similar goals and objectives as the HOC, HACC, CMOC, CIMIC center, or others. These organizations may be referred to by a variety of names or acronyms and are usually established early on and are temporary in nature. No matter the organizational name, the key is providing the link between all relief organizations for the betterment of the affected region(s). Once a HOC, HACC, CMOC, or CIMIC center has been established by the lead relief agency, the coordination role of others diminishes, and functions are accomplished through the normal organization of the JFC's staff. Effective coordination is the key to success, remembering all are ultimately responsible to their own organizations or countries and may have an agenda that does not support the US position, goals, or end state.

CHAPTER III
PLANNING

"Joint operation planning integrates military actions and capabilities with those of other instruments of national power in time, space, and purpose in unified action to achieve the JFC's [joint force commander's] objectives."

JP 5-0, Joint Operation Planning

1. General

a. Joint planners should incorporate CMO into the deliberate and crisis action planning processes. CMO help shape the OE and support the GCC's TCP. In theater campaign planning, CMO enables eventual transition to civilian control after major operations. CMO planners must ensure their input supports the JFC's intent and operational concept. While CMO may not be the main joint force effort through the first four joint operation phases (see Figure III-1), CMO are typically a major part of the latter phases. The termination criteria may rely heavily on successful CMO efforts to establish a stable environment (phase IV) for successful transfer to civil authority (in phase V).

b. **Planning.** The J-9 normally leads the CMO staff element and is an important asset in planning and coordinating CMO. Planning should establish the objectives, MOEs, decisive points, and desired outcomes of the operation or campaign. CMO planning normally conforms to five LOEs: economic stability, infrastructure, public health and welfare, public education and information, and rule of law.

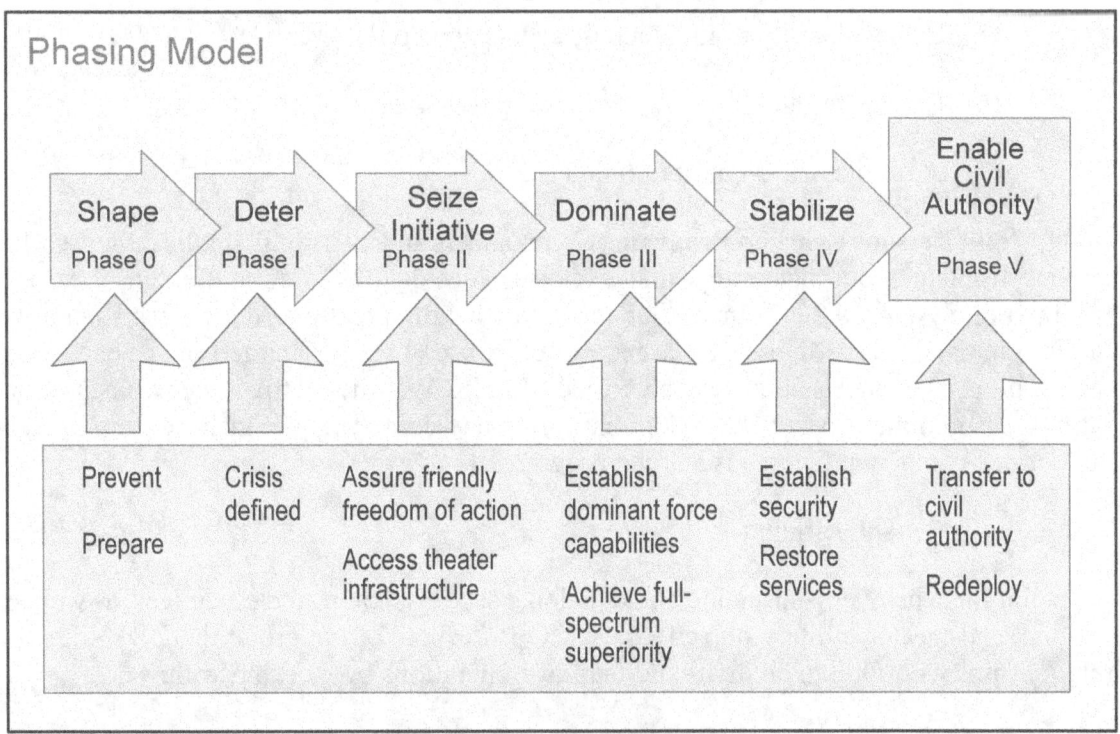

Figure III-1. Phasing Model

c. **Deployment, Employment, Sustainment, and Redeployment Planning.** A clear articulation of CMO mission requirements enhances selection of forces to perform CMO. APEX system integrates all elements of deliberate or crisis action planning and identifies, resources, and time-phasing of required forces. APEX and JOPP promote coherent planning across all levels of war and command echelons. JOPP is a less formal but orderly analytical process that provides a methodical approach to planning before and during joint operations. JOPP focuses on interaction between the commander and his staff, the commanders and staffs of the next higher and lower commands, and supporting commanders and their staffs to develop plans or orders for a specific mission.

For further detail concerning planning, refer to JP 5-0, Joint Operation Planning, *JP 3-33,* Joint Task Force Headquarters, *and JP 3-35,* Deployment and Redeployment Operations.

d. **Post Conflict Operations.** Sustained hostilities can devastate HN and even regional facilities, services, and personnel. US forces and MNFs may be required to distribute emergency food and water, clothing, shelter, and health services supplies to civilians.

e. **Conflict Termination or Consolidation Considerations.** Planning considerations for CMO include:

(1) The post conflict mission objectives.

(2) Integrated military-civilian organizational and oversight elements or agencies.

(3) The extent of devastation.

(4) Local violence and IPI capacity.

(5) The availability of indigenous leaders and civil servants.

(6) The desires and objectives of other governments.

(7) US military in support to failed states.

f. **Joint Lessons Learned Program.** Commanders and their staffs should review CMO lessons from previous operations and exercises located in the Joint Lessons Learned Information System (JLLIS). In turn, upon completion of operations, it is the responsibility of the command to record lessons learned for future use. Lessons learned can be entered at the appropriate unclassified or classified JLLIS website, https://www.jllis.mil or http://jllis.smil.mil, respectively. Additionally, lessons learned may be gleaned from each of the Service component's lessons learned programs.

2. **Planning Considerations**

Joint force planners must understand national security policy and objectives, as well as national and theater military objectives. CMO is designed to improve the US military's relationships with foreign civilians and facilitate operations by working with:

a. HN and regional legal institutions, customs, social relationships, economic organizations, and concepts of human and fundamental rights.

b. Public communications media being controlled, or censored, inconsistently with US standards.

c. Public education.

d. Cultural and religious leaders.

e. Public health and sanitation.

f. Labor, procurement, and contracting leaders.

g. DC care and control, civilian supply, public safety, transportation, and humanitarian relief.

h. Relief or assistance may conflict with local law, religion, or cultural standards.

i. International law, customs, and practice governing the sovereign territory of each nation.

j. The relationship to and use of water, air, and land as it relates to the indigenous populations and environmental security.

k. Ability to communicate with IPI.

l. Criminal activities and the informal economy impacting the economic environment.

m. Competing requirements and agendas of multiple stakeholders. Figure III-2 depicts general planning considerations.

3. Other Planning Considerations

a. **Strategic Guidance.** The adherence to strategic guidance and consistent messaging should be considered when planning information-related capabilities (IRCs) and similar activities of the country team; and may influence and inform the various organizations and partner countries that may be involved in the given operation. The supported GCC and subordinate JFCs should ensure messages are not contradictory or damage the credibility of the joint force or compromise the essential elements of friendly information.

b. **IO**

(1) CMO is designed to engage HN personnel, IGOs, NGOs, and IPI to shape their opinions and subsequent behavior. IO integrates IRCs with other lines of operation (LOOs) to influence, disrupt, corrupt, or usurp adversaries and potential adversaries decision-making processes protecting those of the US.

```
┌─────────────────────────────────────────────────────────────────────────┐
│  Civil-Military Operations General Planning Considerations                │
│                                                                           │
│   ●  Administrative, logistic, and communications support requirements of │
│      civil-military operations (CMO) forces                               │
│                                                                           │
│   ●  The need for early deployment and employment of CMO forces           │
│                                                                           │
│   ●  The coordination between CMO requirements and plans and strategies   │
│                                                                           │
│   ●  The coordination of CMO requirements with other appropriate staff    │
│      functions, the interagency, intergovernmental organizations,         │
│      nongovernmental organizations, host nation, and private sector       │
│                                                                           │
│   ●  Additional lead time normally necessary for Reserve Component forces  │
│      availability                                                         │
│                                                                           │
│   ●  The early identification of CMO resources and task organization to   │
│      support the plan and maximize use of external organizations          │
│                                                                           │
│   ●  Thorough inclusion and coverage of CMO in each phase of the plan     │
│      requires proactive CMO staff work                                    │
│                                                                           │
│   ●  The need to work closely with the intelligence directorate of a joint staff to │
│      both provide and obtain civil environment intelligence used in planning │
│                                                                           │
│   ●  CMO input to the targeting process will help reduce destruction of   │
│      essential civilian capabilities needed in phases IV (Stabilize) and V │
│      (Enable Civil Authorities)                                           │
│                                                                           │
│   ●  The tactical, operational, and strategic objectives achievable via CMO │
│                                                                           │
│   ●  Language, cultural, and social customs for the operational area      │
│                                                                           │
│   ●  The need to work closely with the joint force staff in the collecting and │
│      fusing of civil information to provide the commander with an analysis of the │
│      civil component for use in the planning process                      │
└─────────────────────────────────────────────────────────────────────────┘
```

Figure III-2. Civil-Military Operations General Planning Considerations

(2) IO support CMO by:

(a) Key leader engagement. By establishing and maintaining liaison or dialogue with key HN personnel, NGOs, and IGOs, CMO can potentially secure a more expedient and credible means of disseminating information and influencing behavior.

(b) Informing populace of CMO activities and support.

(c) Correcting misinformation and hostile propaganda directed against HN civilian authorities by adversaries.

(d) Promoting civilian HN legitimacy to the indigenous population.

(e) Providing information to assess CMO operations (e.g., civilian polling data).

(3) **IO Cell.** The JFCs normally **assigns responsibility for IO** to the operations directorate of a joint staff (J-3). The J-3 has primary staff responsibility to plan, coordinate, integrate, and assess IO as part of the overall operation or campaign. **The J-3 may**

designate an IO cell chief. JFC guidance establishes the IO cell's organization and relations with the joint staff, components, and other organizations. **The IO cell should have CMO or CA representation.** The IO cell conducts early and continuous coordination with PA, CA, MISO, and IRCs so messages do not contradict, or damage the JFC, or compromise critical information. An IO cell chief may chair an IO working group.

HAITI INFORMATION OPERATIONS

During Operation UNIFIED RESPONSE, Lieutenant General Keen and his staff also recognized the need to implement an effective strategic communications plan to get out in front of the expanding public media presence. To accomplish this they organized the Joint Interagency Information Cell (JIIC). The JIIC was a centralized, coordination body comprised of US Government departments and agencies, headed up by a JIIC director, and assisted by the US Embassy Public Diplomacy Officer. The communications goal was to ensure key audiences understood the United States' role in the global effort and to portray the US as a capable, efficient, and effective responder. Focusing on the key audiences of the Haitian people, the Haitian leadership, the international community, and the American people, the core themes emphasized "Haitians helping Haitians" and ever-expanding partnerships. Of equal importance was dispelling the undesirable themes that the US was keeping an inept Haitian Government afloat, that it was an occupying force, or that the US would rebuild Haiti. The White House sent a "trusted agent" to Haiti in an effort to synchronize situational awareness and messages, and the Chairman of the Joint Chiefs of Staff, Admiral Mullen, sent his personal public affairs officer to serve with the Joint Task Force Commander. "For the first few days of the crisis, the guy that was most valuable to me was the Chairman of the Joint Chiefs of Staff's Public Affairs Officer (PAO)—he was with me all the time."

Operation UNIFIED RESPONSE—Haiti Earthquake 2010
Assistant Professor David R. DiOrio
Joint Forces Staff College

For more details concerning IO, refer to JP 3-13, Information Operations.

   c. **PA**

      (1) The mission of joint PA is to plan, coordinate, and synchronize US military public information, command information, and community engagement activities and resources to support the commander's objectives through the communication of truthful, timely, and factual unclassified information about joint military activities within the operational area to foreign, domestic, and internal audiences.

      (2) Media coverage of CMO impacts perceptions of success or failure and may influence the commanders' decisions.

(3) PA, coordinated with other military (e.g., MNFs) and nonmilitary (e.g., DOS) communication, can shape the OE, prevent misinformation and disinformation from inciting protest or hostilities, and help establish or maintain political and public support to achieve the commander's objectives.

(a) Proper staff coordination is required to ensure information released by one staff element does not conflict with or complicate the work of another. For example, PA, CMO, and MIS messages may be different and may even be aimed at different target audiences, but they must not contradict one another, or the credibility of one or all three may be lost or compromised. This coordination should take place during the planning process.

(b) PA support to CMO may include:

<u>1</u>. Coordinate releases to the media with all appropriate agencies to facilitate consistent and accurate information flow to the local population.

<u>2</u>. Develop and disseminate media releases about CMO efforts to local, national, and international media, as well as to command information outlets.

<u>3</u>. Help media cover CMO or CAO. Highlighting HN government, military, civilian group, or organization contributions to joint operations may prove most beneficial to US interests.

<u>4</u>. In cooperation with CA, publish and broadcast information to protect DCs.

<u>5</u>. Clearly state US objectives and US intent to transition operations to HN agencies or NGOs (in the case of FHA operations) as soon as conditions permit. Highlighting US intent to assist until the HN government or NGOs can lead operations supports the exlt strategy.

<u>6</u>. The JFC and PAO are the primary official military spokespersons.

(4) The Joint Public Affairs Support Element (JPASE), a joint subordinate command of the United States Transportation Command's Joint Enabling Capabilities Command, provides ready, rapidly deployable joint PA capability to CCDRs in order to facilitate rapid establishment of joint force headquarters, bridge joint PA requirements, and conduct PA training to meet theater challenges. The criticality of PA during CMO places considerable strain on existing PA staffs, which JPASE can augment during the planning and execution of CMO.

For further details concerning PA, refer to JP 3-61, Public Affairs.

d. **Legal**

(1) Legal advisors should work with both the planning and operations directorates to review and prepare plans and orders, as well as agreements or memoranda of understanding between US forces and HN or nonmilitary organizations. Many CMO

staffs will have a CA legal team to plan and provide legal analysis. The SJA provides legal expertise whether or not a CA legal team is available.

(2) CA legal teams or SJAs advice and assist during preparation and review of CMO plans for consistency with US law, SecDef guidance, and the rules and principles of international law, including treaties, other international agreements, and local and HN laws. The CMO staff element provides input for the development of rules of engagement (ROE). CMO missions may warrant supplemental ROE.

(3) CA legal teams and SJAs provide predeployment training to personnel and units preparing to conduct CMO. This training should include:

(a) Law of war.

(b) Human Rights Violations and Reporting Requirements. Personnel should be trained in the law of war to recognize and report violations to their chain of command.

(c) ROE.

(d) Status of Forces. The status of forces is an important concern for CMO planners. Numerous legal issues such as HN criminal and civil jurisdiction, authority to conduct LE activities, claims against the US or US personnel, authority for US forces to carry arms and use force, FP, entry and exit requirements, customs and tax liability, contracting authority, authority to provide health care without a local medical license, vehicle registration and licensing, communications support, facilities for US forces, contractor status (local, US or other nationals), authority to detain or arrest, as well as identify vetting and provisions for transferring custody should be resolved prior to deployment. The SJA provides legal advice concerning status of forces issues, to include the provisions of current agreements, the need for additional agreements, and the procedures for obtaining agreements.

(e) Environmental law issues.

(4) During combat operations, CA legal teams provide the JFC analysis and recommendations concerning population control measures; minimizing collateral damage or injury to the civilian population; treatment of DCs, civilian internees, and detainees; acquisition of private and public property for military purposes; MISO and IO; and other operational law matters.

(5) During the stabilization phase, CA legal teams may provide legal services concerning claims submitted by local civilians and FHA issues.

(6) The JFC's SJA and the CA SJA may advice and assist on matters related to civil administration. SJAs also may provide counsel regarding the creation and supervision of military tribunals and other activities for administration of civil law and order. The JFC may require legal services with respect to HN jurisdiction over US military personnel and activities. Figure III-3 highlights legal issues that may influence joint force operations.

```
Legal Issues

  Military Justice
    • Uniformity versus efficiency
    • Courts-martial asset sharing
    • Divergent command philosophies
    • Chain of command

  Claims
    • Foreign claims
    • Single-service claims authority

  Legal Assistance
    • Asset utilization and interoperability

  Environmental Law
    • Applicability of US law abroad
    • Environmental treaties and agreements

  Fiscal Law/Contracts
    • Fiscal authority to supply logistic support
    • Contingency contracting and host-nation support

  International Law
    • Treaties and customary international law
    • Law of armed conflict
    • National policy issues
    • Executive orders
    • Status-of-forces agreement/status of mission agreements

  Operations Law Issues
    • Overflight of national airspace
    • Freedom of navigation
    • Basing rights (intermediate staging bases and forward operations bases)
    • Dislocated civilians
    • Humanitarian assistance
    • Use of deadly force

  Rules of Engagement (ROE)/Rules for the Use of Force (RUF)
    • An operations responsibility
    • Legal advisor may be the most experienced and educated in ROE/RUF
      development
```

Figure III-3. Legal Issues

For more details concerning legal matters, refer to JP 1-04, Legal Support to Military Operations.

e. **Mortuary Affairs**

(1) In CMO, the death of civilians requires specific political and cultural sensitivities. CA can help the JFC avoid diplomatic or political and cultural complications.

(2) CA can act as intermediaries between the affected organization and the families to ensure the command honors cultural traditions and complies with local national regulations.

(3) CA can assist local agencies interface with military assets providing support to remove the remains. This can include handling customs, location of storage facilities, burial sites, transportation options, and providing linguists.

(4) CA advise the command on cultural traditions relating to the handling and removing of remains.

For further guidance on mortuary affairs, refer to JP 4-06, Mortuary Affairs.

f. **Intelligence.** Joint intelligence preparation of the operational environment's (JIPOE's) continuous process defines the total OE; describes the impact of the OE (to include the civil and cultural environment); evaluates the adversary; and determines and describes adversary potential COAs (particularly the adversary's most likely COA and the COA most dangerous to friendly forces and mission accomplishment). The JIPOE process assists JFCs and their staffs in achieving information superiority by identifying adversary COGs, focusing intelligence collection at the right time and place, and analyzing the impact of the OE on military operations.

For more information on JIPOE, see JP 2-01.3, Joint Intelligence Preparation of the Operational Environment.

g. **Engineering.** CMO will likely rely on engineering for construction, repair, operations, and maintenance of national, regional, and local infrastructure and essential services to include facilities, water, sanitation, transportation, electricity and fuel distribution. The joint staff engineers should be integrated into CMO planning throughout the entire process to synchronize engineer planning with CMO objectives and provide engineering technical expertise. The staff engineers can provide initial technical assessments of critical infrastructure and basic services necessary to sustain the population. They can also plan and coordinate follow-on infrastructure surveys as part of the overall civil reconnaissance (CR) plan to provide detailed descriptions on the condition of major services. These assessments and surveys will generally follow the model of sewage, water, electricity, academics, trash, medical, security, and other considerations. The engineer planning may include developing and managing construction projects, using military or contract means, to improve infrastructure and services. Engineer planning can include the United States Army Corps of Engineers (USACE), Naval Facilities Engineering Command (NAVFAC), USAID, HN government agencies, and other NGOs and IGOs. The joint civil-military engineering board, CMOC, and the JIACG can facilitate coordination between stakeholders to improve planning and execution of engineering.

For more information on military engineer capabilities, see JP 3-34, Joint Engineer Operations.

h. **Logistics**

(1) Logistic planners should assess CMO logistic requirements and HN and theater support capabilities. Risks and logistic objectives also should be identified. Emphasis should be placed upon locating logistic bases as close as possible to the recipients. Logistic planners should avoid locating distribution points in major population centers to reduce displacement of large civilians. All potential supply sources should be considered, including HN, commercial, multinational, and pre-positioned supplies. Logistics and support infrastructure to sustain CMO are frequently underestimated. CMO often are logistics and engineering intensive. Therefore, the overall logistic concept should be closely tied into the operational strategy and be mutually supporting. This includes:

(a) Identifying time-phased material requirements, facilities, and other resources. Remote and austere locations may require deployment of materials handling equipment and pre-positioned stocks.

(b) Identifying support methods and procedures required to meet air, land, and sea lines of communications. This also will require plans to deconflict civil and military transportation systems.

(c) Establishing procedures for coordinating and controlling material movements to and within the operational area. Priorities may be established using apportionment systems, providing the commander flexibility to reinforce priority efforts with additional assets.

(2) Planning should include logistic support normally outside military logistics, such as support to the civilian populace (e.g., women, children, and the elderly). CMO often provide support to these categories of individuals, and joint force planners should ensure proper aid is administered.

(3) Joint planners should consider potential requirements to support nonmilitary personnel (e.g., NGOs, IGOs, IPI, and the private sector).

(4) Cultural considerations for logistic planners supporting CMO include:

(a) Inappropriate foods, materials, and methods may have a detrimental impact on CMO operations or the local populace's perception on the legitimacy and professionalism of US forces. Procurement of culturally appropriate foods and materials may require additional planning and coordination or use of contractors.

(b) Cultural heritage sites and property (world heritage monuments, archaeological sites, artifacts, and sites of local significance) should be protected from construction and heavy machinery operations.

i. **Project Management.**
Project management includes planning, organizing, securing, and managing resources to complete goals and objectives. A project is a temporary endeavor constrained by time, funding, and scope. Projects can improve employment, social conditions, and HN legitimacy.

j. **Contracting.** Most theater support contracts are awarded to local vendors and provide employment opportunities to indigenous personnel, promote goodwill with the local populace, and improve the local economic base. Unemployment can lead to unrest and contribute to local support to an insurgency. Maximizing local hires through theater support contracting or civil augmentation programs can alleviate this situation. Expertise and equipment may have to be outsourced. In these instances, social, political, and economic factors must be analyzed before selecting a foreign contractor. One of the ways to mitigate the impact of a foreign contractor is to require they fill a specified percentage of their unskilled labor jobs with local population. In areas where security is an issue, hiring a local security contingent that has a vested interest in the success of the project can prove successful.

(1) **Contracting support plans may need to include specific CMO related guidance such as directives to maximize theater support contracts or local hires.**

(2) **Integrating contracting efforts to the civil-military aspects of the campaign plan.** Integrating contracting support into the civil-military aspects of the GCCs campaign or operation plan requires close coordination between the lead contracting activity, normally a Service, and the GCCs' plans and operations staff. Reconstruction and transition to civil authorities' related contracting effort is normally in support of the COM or NGOs.

(a) **Management Challenges. Joint staff directorates and supporting organizations can be quickly overwhelmed in their dual mission to coordinate forces support and support to civil authorities.** A contracting board which works with project managers can alleviate the challenges of contract requirements.

(b) **Assessing and Balancing Risk to Forces Support.** Another major challenge in planning for and executing contracting support in support of CMO is identifying both the potential risk CMO may cause to overall force support and any potential positive results toward achieving the civil-military objectives. What may be good for forces support may not meet the needs of the civil-military aspects of the overall plan. In all cases, both the increased security risks and contract management requirements must be closely analyzed prior to making any formal decisions.

(c) **Balancing Contracting Business Practices with Operational Needs.** The JFC planners should work closely with the lead Service or joint contracting personnel to balance acceptable contracting business practices and operational requirements.

For further detail concerning logistics and contracting, refer to JP 1-06, Financial Management Support in Joint Operations, *JP 3-33,* Joint Task Force Headquarters, *JP 3-34,* Joint Engineer Operations, *JP 4-0,* Joint Logistics, *and JP 4-10,* Operational Contract Support.

k. **Financial Management**

(1) Financial management supports the JFC through resource management (RM) and finance support. The joint force director for force structure, resource, and assessment or comptroller integrates RM and finance support. Financial management objectives include:

(a) Providing mission-essential funding using the proper source and authority.

(b) Reducing the negative impact of insufficient funding on readiness.

(c) Implementing internal controls to assure fiscal year integrity and to prevent antideficiency violations.

(d) Ensure financial management is coordinated between Services and CCMDs to provide and sustain resources.

(2) Financial managers may be collocated with the joint force SJA and logistic officer to obtain legal opinions and consolidate efforts in the use of JFC's fiscal resources.

(3) Resource managers develop command resource requirements, identify sources of funding, determine costs, acquire funds, distribute and control funds, track costs and obligations, capture costs, conduct reimbursement procedures, establish an internal control process, and coordinate finance support which may include banking and currency support, financial analysis and recommendations, and funding.

For further detail pertaining to financial management, refer to JP 1-06, Financial Management Support in Joint Operations.

l. **IM. Information is shared to build common understanding of challenges and potential solutions. This goal is achieved through proper management of the information and people, processes, and technology.** Information sharing in CMO allows the exchange of information with the interagency and MNF partners and with other organizations (IGOs, NGOs, the private sector). However, that information sharing requires not only close coordination with the foreign disclosure officer and strict adherence to foreign disclosure guidelines, but also knowledge of security classification guides and information security policy and procedures to ensure classified and controlled unclassified information is safeguarded. The information management plan must provide explicit guidance for all forms of information and sharing. Sharing and receiving intelligence information is one of the most difficult aspects of information sharing and requires careful review and handling.

For more details on IM, refer to JP 3-0, Joint Operations, *and JP 3-33,* Joint Task Force Headquarters. *Guidance regarding disclosure of classified military information to foreign governments is contained in DODD 5230.11,* Disclosure of Classified Military Information to Foreign Governments and International Organizations. *Guidance regarding safeguarding, marking, and handling of DOD information (classified, controlled unclassified, and unclassified) is contained in Department of Defense Manual (DODM) 5200.01, Volumes 1-4,* DOD Information Security Program.

m. **Communications**

(1) Communication with USG departments and agencies, MNF, HN and FN agencies, NGOs, IGOs, IPI, the private sector, and other organizations is essential to successful CMO. Communication with stakeholders can include secure and nonsecure

modes using voice, data, and video teleconferencing through a combination of military and commercial systems.

(2) Communications systems are vital to plan, execute, and sustain CMO. Operations, logistic, and intelligence functions depend on communications. Communications is the central system that ties together all aspects of joint operations and allows commanders to maintain C2 of their forces. Communications architecture supporting CMO should provide for interoperable and compatible systems to support the exchange of information among all participants. Direct communications between commanders, interagency partners, NGOs, IGOs, HN, and the private sector facilitates coordination and decision making. While IM should optimize information sharing among participants, it also requires information protection for secure and nonsecure communications. Additionally, communications planning must consider the transition or termination of US involvement and the transfer of responsibility to an IGO, or the HN.

(3) **Spectrum Management.** HNs maintain strict control of spectrum management within their borders, and access by US forces is not guaranteed. CMO require communications and network planners to collaborate with spectrum managers to coordinate frequency allocation to military, government, nongovernmental, and private sector users. Aircraft and weapon systems, especially sensors, consume significant frequency resources in an already congested electromagnetic environment.

(4) **Interoperability.** Nonmilitary agencies may have their own communications networks, and the degree of sophistication will vary. These may include commercial leased circuits and satellite services, and high frequency radio equipment. Commercial satellite services can provide worldwide voice, data, and facsimile communications. This system can provide an excellent communications link between both military and nonmilitary organizations. CMOCs should be equipped with communication equipment that facilitates coordination with all participants. CMOC communications requirements should be identified early. Deployment planners should use commercial off-the-shelf equipment to meet end-user requirements. The need for interoperability of communications equipment in CMO also may necessitate using unclassified communications means during the operation. However, this can create information sharing challenges due to the lack of secure communications. The key to success is evaluating the use of all available means of communicating (military, commercial, HN, and FN) to put together a network that supports CMO. Every situation is unique.

For further details on communications support and spectrum management, refer to JP 6-0, Joint Communications System, *and JP 6-01,* Joint Electromagnetic Spectrum Management Operations.

n. **Information Security.** Information security is the protection of information and information systems against unauthorized access or modification of information, whether in storage, processing, or transit, and against denial of service to authorized users. Communications may be secured against monitoring through encryption. Physical hardening and redundancy reduce system failures stemming from sabotage and elements of nature.

Coordination with other agencies (e.g., interagency partners and non-US organizations) and MNFs also complicates communications security.

o. **Religious Affairs**

(1) While it may not be the primary catalyst for war, religion can be a contributing factor. Some examples include:

(a) Invoking religious overtones to develop an exclusivist vision and program for national and international action.

(b) Using a government's or a group's religion as a motivating factor for socializing conflict.

(c) Linking ideologies with theological concepts that have mass appeal; conflicts "theologized" to justify existence, establish legitimacy, gain popularity, and enact policies, laws, and COAs for internal and external activities.

(d) Attaining an end being gained by using theological concepts as a means to that end.

(2) **By recognizing the significance of religion, cultural sensitivities, and ideology held by allies, multinational partners, and adversaries,** JFCs may avoid unintentionally alienating friendly military forces or civilian populations that could hamper military operations. Commanders and their staffs should also consider religion, other cultural issues, and ideology while planning CMO. Chaplains shall not participate in activities that might compromise their noncombatant status under the Geneva Conventions, nor shall they function as intelligence collectors. However, the joint force chaplain (JFCH), as a staff officer, will participate as appropriate in planning for the impact of religion on current and future operations.

(3) As directed by the JFC, in coordination with the CMOC, and in consultation with the CCMD chaplain, a JFCH may also conduct liaison with key civilian religious leaders and faith-based organizations, with the goal of fostering understanding and reconciliation.

For more details concerning religious support, refer to JP 1-05, Religious Affairs in Joint Operations.

p. **Linguist Support.** CMO planners should determine linguist support requirements by phase. If needs in this area exceed organic capabilities, services can be provided by other USG departments and agencies as well as through contracts.

q. **CA Planning Considerations**

(1) Successful accomplishment of CAO in large part depends on adequate plans and policy determinations, an adequate staff capability, and availability of dedicated CA to assist the commander in carrying out responsibilities for CMO. It is important that CA be

concentrated on those tasks that are most likely to lead to mission accomplishment. CA forces provide military commanders the knowledge and analytical/operational capabilities for CA-related decisions and actions that promote achievement of military objectives and facilitate transition to civilian authority.

(2) During the joint planning process, CA should:

(a) Identify CMO administrative, logistic, and communications support requirements.

(b) Recommend CMO force deployment schedules.

(c) Coordinate CMO with other staff functions and outside agencies.

(d) Provide COAs for JCMOTF development.

For further details on CA planning, refer to Appendix B, "Planning Considerations for Civil Affairs Operations."

Intentionally Blank

CHAPTER IV
CIVIL AFFAIRS FORCES AND CIVIL AFFAIRS OPERATIONS

"Over the long term, we cannot kill or capture our way to victory… operations should be subordinate to measures that promote better governance, economic programs…and efforts to address grievances among the discontented from which the terrorists recruit."

Secretary of Defense Robert M. Gates, National Defense University, 29 September 2008

1. General

a. CA forces conduct military engagement, HCA, and NA to influence HN and FN populations. CA specialize in indirect approaches in support of traditional warfare (e.g., stability operations), and IW. CA are population-oriented rather than focused on enemy combatants. Additionally, CA analyze and report civil sector input to the COP.

b. CA are organized, trained, equipped, and deployed to work with IPI and other interagency partners, IGOs, and NGOs in support of the JFC's objectives and military end state. Conventional US forces may also routinely conduct CMO.

c. CA forces assess the civil environment; identify and engage with key authorities and other influential civilians; build civil relationships; identify factors fostering instability; and conduct CAO to achieve JFC objectives or build partnership capacity in support of strategic goals.

d. CA forces assess impacts of the population and culture on military operations; assess impact of military operations on the population and culture; and facilitate interorganizational coordination to:

(1) Improve relations between joint forces and civilian authorities.

(2) Provide civil considerations to the COP.

(3) Plan, and conduct population-oriented, indirect approaches to joint and USG operations.

(4) Integrate civil-military teams to support military engagement and security cooperation activities in support of USG operations and objectives.

(5) Improve USG partnerships with HN governments and their populations.

e. CA personnel can help integrate population-oriented approaches to joint operations, and build USG interagency relationships. They also support specialized activities such as support to US embassy country teams and various theater security cooperation activities.

f. CA personnel can provide regional, cultural, and linguistic expertise to support interorganizational coordination, including:

(1) Plan, advise, and assist the joint force to create and implement civil security or civil capacity building programs or institutions for HN government or security forces.

(2) Providing CA expertise in support of CMO for joint forces engaged in military operations.

g. At the tactical, operational, and strategic levels, CA forces are the main conduit for the joint force to engage, other interagency and multinational partners, IGOs, NGOs, and HN. CA forces can operate a CMOC or form the nucleus of a JCMOTF.

h. CA forces support USG programs to build partner capacity, to include governance, economic development, public health welfare, infrastructure, rule of law, and public education and information. These programs are primarily applicable to the strategic and operational levels, and are executed primarily during routine security cooperation and military engagement activities.

i. In the absence of a legitimate HN civilian authority, CA forces help the joint force execute governmental functions. CA functional specialists prepare for transition to HN governance. CA units provide assessments on local, regional, and national governments, help establish local governance, and encourage the local population to accept HN governance.

See JP 3-07, Stability Operations.

2. Civil Affairs Responsibilities

CA joint responsibilities (see Figure IV-1) are not sequential but may be conducted throughout all phases of operations.

3. Civil Affairs Forces

a. CAO manage relations between military forces and civil authorities through coordination with other USG departments and agencies, IGOs, NGOs, IPI, and the private sector. They involve CA functional specialty skills that are normally the responsibility of HN governments. All CMO should support the JFC's intent.

b. CA can support both SOF and CF. CA units supporting conventional and SOF units execute the same core tasks.

c. CA teams are trained to identify critical civil vulnerabilities, conduct CR, engage HN and interagency counterparts, create country or region-specific supporting plans, develop a series of activities to foster unity of effort to achieve JFC objectives, oversee CMO projects, and conduct transition activities. CA units can serve as primary CMO advisors and joint force representatives to the HN government, and interorganizational partners.

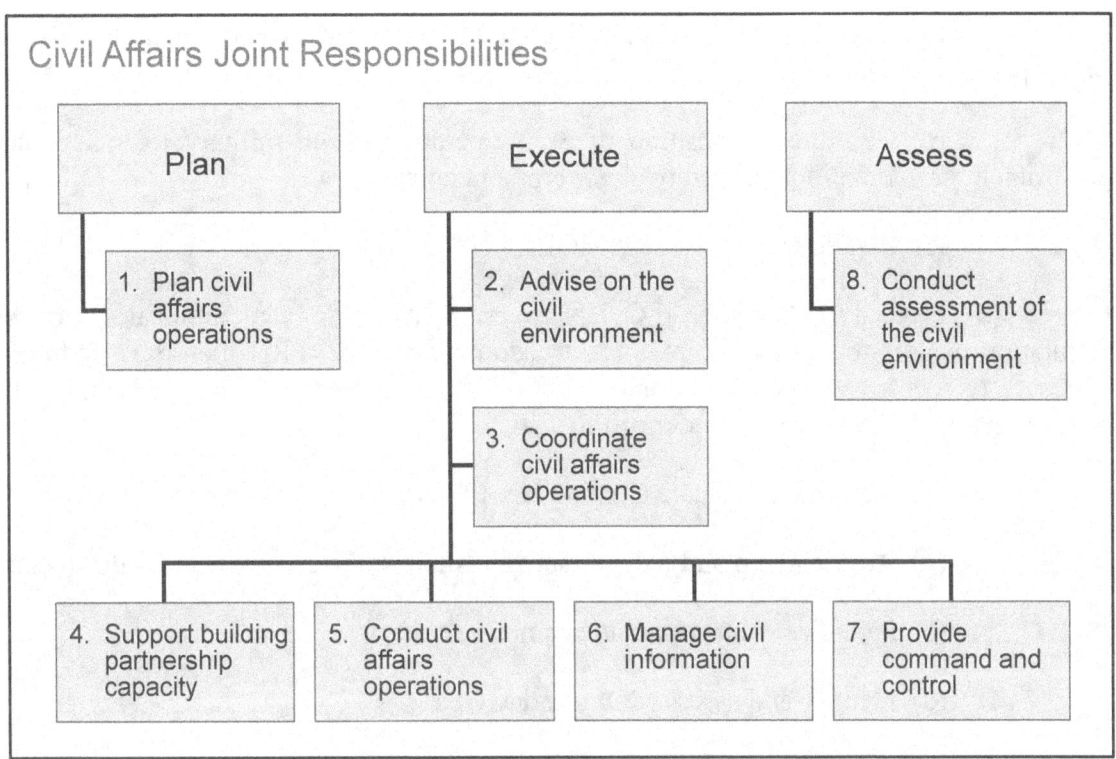

Figure IV-1. Civil Affairs Joint Responsibilities

d. CA forces enhance JFC ability to execute stability operations, IW, and military transitional authority. CA forces functional specialist teams help stabilize or restore the local civil environment. These teams are organized into sections for governance, economic stability, infrastructure, rule of law, public health and welfare, and public education and information. The functional specialist team advises, assists, restores, implements, or enables transition of basic governmental functions. They also coordinate with USG interagency partners to enable a whole-of-government approach to stabilizing the civil environment.

For more information, refer to Appendix A, "Service Capabilities."

4. Characteristics of Civil Affairs Operations

a. CAO are actions to coordinate with HN military and civilian agencies, other government departments and agencies, NGOs, or IGOs, to support US policy or the commander's assigned mission.

b. CA core tasks include:

(1) **SCA.** CA supports continuity of government in an HN. CA tasks are to

(a) Identify, validate, or evaluate HN essential service infrastructure and capabilities.

(b) Assess the needs of the IPI in terms of the CA functional areas of expertise.

(c) Liaison between military and civilian agencies.

(d) Coordinate and synchronize collaborative interagency or multinational SCA operations.

(e) Coordinate transition of SCA operations from military to indigenous government or international transitional government control.

(f) Conduct CIM to assess MOEs.

(2) **PRC.** PRC helps the JFC, HN governments, or de facto authorities manage population centers to enhance joint force freedom of action. PRC identifies, reduces, relocates, or accesses the population and resources that may impede or otherwise threaten joint operations. CA tasks in support of PRC:

(a) Identify or evaluate existing HN PRC measures and capabilities.

(b) Advise and plan PRC measures to support the commander's objectives.

(c) Publicize control measures among IPI.

(d) Identify and assess MOEs and MOPs.

(e) Execute of selected PRC operations.

(f) Assist in the arbitration of problems arising from the implementation of PRC measures.

(g) Conduct targeted CIM in support of PRC.

(3) **FHA.** CA forces administer aspects of FHA in coordination with interagency partners. CA tasks:

(a) Prepare and review contingency plans to assist USG departments and agencies, IGOs, HN agencies, and NGOs to support FHA.

(b) Monitor all FHA operations for compliance with law, agreements, and treaties.

(c) Review guidance from DOD and the GCC regarding FHA operations in TCPs, FHA and disaster relief plans, and foreign consequence management (FCM) plans.

(d) Assess the environments in which US forces will conduct FHA:

1. Political situation.

2. Physical boundaries of the area.

3. Potential threat to forces and IPI.

4. Global visibility of the situation.

<u>5.</u> Media interest climate for FHA operations.

<u>6.</u> Assess social and cultural factors that may influence FHA delivery and effectiveness.

(e) Confirm and validate HN's ability to manage HA in the JOA.

(f) Establish a CMOC to coordinate CAO and CMO efforts with interagency and multinational HA efforts in the JOA.

(g) Identify HA resources, including government agencies, military units, NGOs, and IPI; and establish contact and work relationships.

(h) Assess, monitor, and report the impact of FHA operations on the populace and the populace on the operations.

(i) Develop strategy to mitigate negative political, economic, legal, social, and military perceptions associated with FHA operations.

(j) Target CIM to support information sharing with partners.

(4) **NA.** CA tasks:

(a) Identify, validate, or evaluate NA project nominations.

(b) Train HN military to plan and execute CMO and CAO.

(c) Track costs to execute NA projects.

(d) Provide quality control assessments of NA operations and costs.

(e) Target CIM to assess MOEs.

(5) **CIM.** Civil information is developed from data about civil areas, structures, capabilities, organizations, people, and events (ASCOPE) that can be fused or processed to increase interagency, IGO, and NGO situational awareness. CIM is a CA planning consideration. CIM is the process whereby civil information is gathered, analyzed, and entered into a central database, and fused with the supported JFC, higher headquarters, DOD and joint intelligence organizations, other USG departments and agencies, interagency partners, NGOs, and the private sector to ensure the timely availability of information for analysis and the widest possible dissemination of the raw and analyzed civil information to military and nonmilitary partners.

See Appendix C, "Civil Information Management," for additional details on CIM.

(6) Generally, CA tasks:

(a) Inform the COP.

(b) Track civil metrics on MOP/MOE.

(c) Inform the commander's critical information requirement (CCIR) development process.

(d) Synchronize operations throughout the OE.

(e) Identify civil named areas of interest.

(f) Maintain a historical account of an AOR through all phases.

5. Civil Affairs Operations and the Range of Military Operations

a. CAO support military operations and vary in size, purpose, and intensity within a range that extends from military engagement, security cooperation, and deterrence activities to crisis response and limited contingency operations, and, if necessary, major operations and campaigns. The nature of the security environment may require CA forces to engage in several types of joint operations simultaneously across the range of military operations. Whether the prevailing context for the operation is one of traditional warfare or IW, or even if the operation takes place outside of war, combat and stabilization are not sequential or alternative operations. The CA planner and CMO staff plan, integrate, and synchronize with other operations to facilitate unity of effort and effective use of developmental resources.

b. CA forces provide the JFC an analysis of the local populace's perceptions, their willingness to support US and friendly forces, and other information related to CMO. CA forces promote military objectives and transition to civil authorities.

c. Joint force planners should consider CMO in all phases and balance offensive, defensive, and stability operations. Over emphasis on offensive and defensive operations in earlier phases, to the exclusion of stability operations, may limit development of basic transition planning.   Even during sustained combat operations, civil security and humanitarian relief must be established or restored as areas are occupied, bypassed, or returned to a transitional authority or HN control.

d. Initial CAO should advise the JFC and develop plans to establish civil security to protect both the joint force and the civilian population while meeting the humanitarian needs of HN civilians affected by armed conflict. Simultaneously, the JFC should work with partners to support the restoration of essential services and to repair and protect critical infrastructure. CAO may best serve JFC objectives when conducted in areas where the USG interagency, IGOs, and NGOs cannot operate.

e. Joint forces robust C2 and logistics capabilities may make the JFC the only viable USG entity to execute operations in hostile environments. CAO should plan and support transition of civil activities to interagency partners, HN, or IPI. The lead agency may not have the capacity to execute civil administrative and other stability functions. CA forces should support the HN government through SCA or execute government functions through a transitional military authority. The joint force may be the only USG entity capable of civil administration, stabilization, and reconstruction efforts until after combat objectives are accomplished.

f. During crisis response and limited contingency operations, the combination of stability, offensive, and defensive operations varies with the circumstances. Many crisis response and limited contingency operations, such as FHA, may not require combat. Others, such as strikes and raids, may not require stability operations. Still others, such as COIN, will require a delicate balance of stability, offensive, and defensive operations. CAO may be executed by CAPTs or functional specialty teams at the strategic and operational level or via the execution of direct support by tactical CA teams in the JOA. The JFC may determine that the operating environment for a crisis response supports the creation of a JCMOTF. In this case, the senior CA officer and the CA officer's staff may form the nucleus of the task force C2 and be augmented by supporting units to respond to the crisis.

For further detail, refer to JP 3-07, Stability Operations.

g. COIN is comprehensive civilian and military efforts taken to defeat an insurgency and to address underlying causes of instability. COIN requires joint forces to fight and build sequentially or simultaneously depending on the circumstances. CAO are fundamental to COIN. In the COIN process of clear, hold, and build, CAO are essential. CAO provide direct support to tactical units during the clear phase. During the hold phase, CAO are targeted to isolate insurgents from the populace while simultaneously building partner capacity.

For further detail on COIN, refer to JP 3-24, Counterinsurgency Operations.

h. During military engagement, security cooperation, and deterrence activities, CAO conducted in consonance with the GCC's TCP objectives enable joint operations and support individual country teams. CA support to stabilization efforts during peacetime can take the form of NA operations and directed SCA.

i. Sustained joint force presence in a region can promote a secure environment in which diplomatic, economic, and informational programs designed to reduce the drivers of conflict and instability can flourish. Joint force presence and CMO can prevent unstable situations from escalating into larger conflicts.

j. Joint forces normally conduct NA and other military engagement, security cooperation, and deterrence activities in relatively stable states. NA activities, USG efforts to build partner capacity and security sector reform (SSR) are designed to build regional security. US forces stabilization efforts outside of war or crisis response generally focus on SSR.

k. DODI 3000.05, *Stability Operations,* directs DOD to develop, implement, and operate civil-military teams to support CMO activities for infrastructure reconstruction, governance, security, economic stability, and capacity development.

l. DOS, USAID, the United States Institute of Peace, and the US Army Peacekeeping and Stability Operations Institute published guidelines for civil-military teams for USG interagency consideration.

For further detail on civil-military teaming, refer to JP 3-08, Interorganizational Coordination During Joint Operations.

6. Civil Affairs Participation in the Joint Operation Planning Process

a. When operational considerations require CMO staff supervision of related processes, activities, and capabilities associated with basic joint functions, the commander may establish a J-9 and staff it with a CA-qualified officer. Stability operations, FHA, IW, CAO, and operational commands with forces in countries under Title 22, USC, authority require additional coordination and planning prior to deployment. Commanders may elect to establish a JCMOTF in lieu of building an internal staff.

b. The J-9 coordinates all CMO activities through the CMOC, which is the focal point for all partner engagements not formally organized within the chain of command. The J-9 maintains visibility of and manages the civilian component of the COP. This requires input from sources outside of military and HN. CMOC operations and inclusion of information from these varied sources contribute to the accuracy and timeliness of the COP and it communicates an indigenous perspective (e.g., availability of essential services and the subsequent second and third order effects). The CMOC can work in parallel, in conjunction with, or independently of the JIACG within defined roles and responsibilities.

c. The J-9 requests representation for CMO/CAO-specific meetings and assigns representatives to other established meetings that address the basic joint functions, which include, but are not limited to, the following:

(1) JIPOE.

(2) Joint targeting coordination board.

(3) J-3 current/future operations.

(4) Plans directorate of a joint staff.

(5) Commanders update brief.

(6) CCIR development process.

(7) Joint civil-military engineering board.

d. The J-9 advises the commander on CMO and specified supporting CAO to accomplish mission objectives. The J-9 identifies relevant aspects of the civil component of the environment and validates that CR tasks satisfy the collection plan, enhance CIM, and support answering open CCIRs.

e. The J-9 participates in both lethal and nonlethal operational planning and targeting. The J-9 provides guidance on phasing and synchronizing complementary combat, CMO, and CAO.

f. The J-9's participation in the IO working group helps to validate that subordinate plans promote established themes and messages and they synchronize operations with higher headquarters intent. Additionally, the J-9 recommends that CCIRs incorporate recommended PIRs related to civil aspects of the JOA identified during planning.

g. Depending upon the level of CMO/CAO activities, the J-9 can be scaled to meet the required level of interaction.

(1) Light. The light manning configuration for a geographic CCMD or TSOC CA J-9 section provides the commander minimum capability to advise and plan during operational engagements or contingency operations. It enables the commander to maintain minimal level of situational awareness of the civil dimensions in the AOR and allows civil information coordination with key staff sections. The disadvantages of this configuration lie in the low personnel density, which affects the ability to coordinate quickly with other staff sections and components. Additional manning augmentation is required to deal with unexpected contingency or FHA operations (see Figure IV-2).

(2) Medium. The medium staffing configuration for a geographic CCMD or TSOC CA J-9 section allows the commander to increase the staff's coordination ability for CMO and CAO, greatly increases the commander's awareness on the civil dimensions of the AOR, and allows greater staff flexibility when dealing with current operations. Dedicated personnel increases awareness and integration of CMO and CAO into geographic CCMD or TSOC activities and enhances integration of the civil dimension into ongoing efforts with the staff and interagency partners (Figure IV-3).

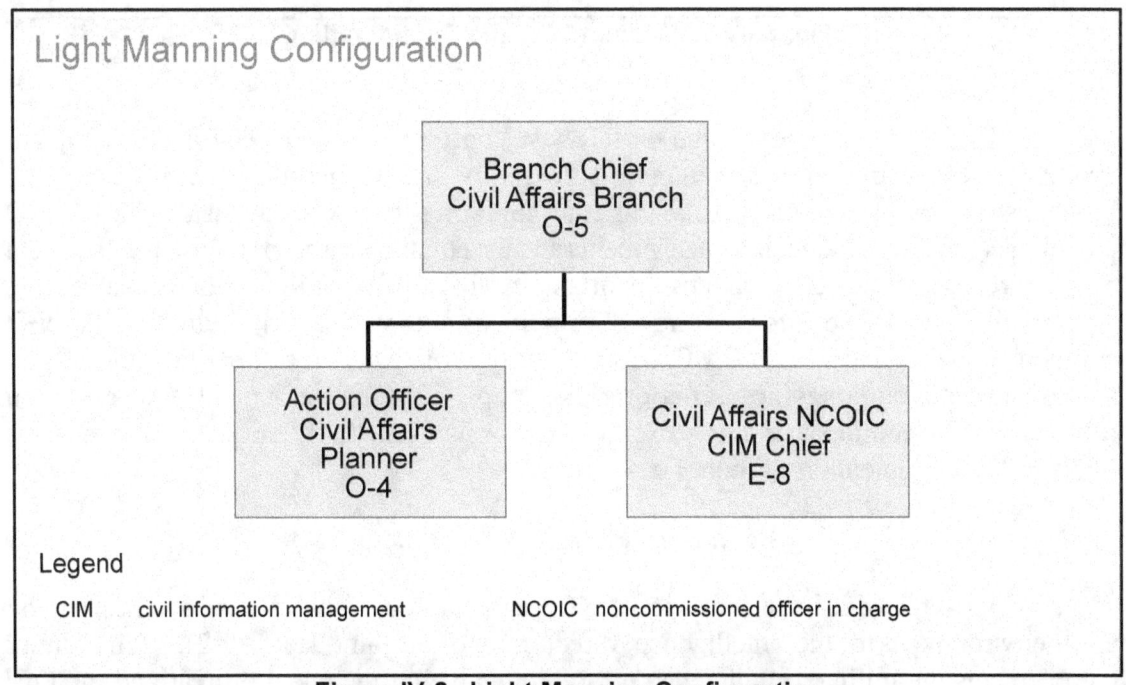

Figure IV-2. Light Manning Configuration

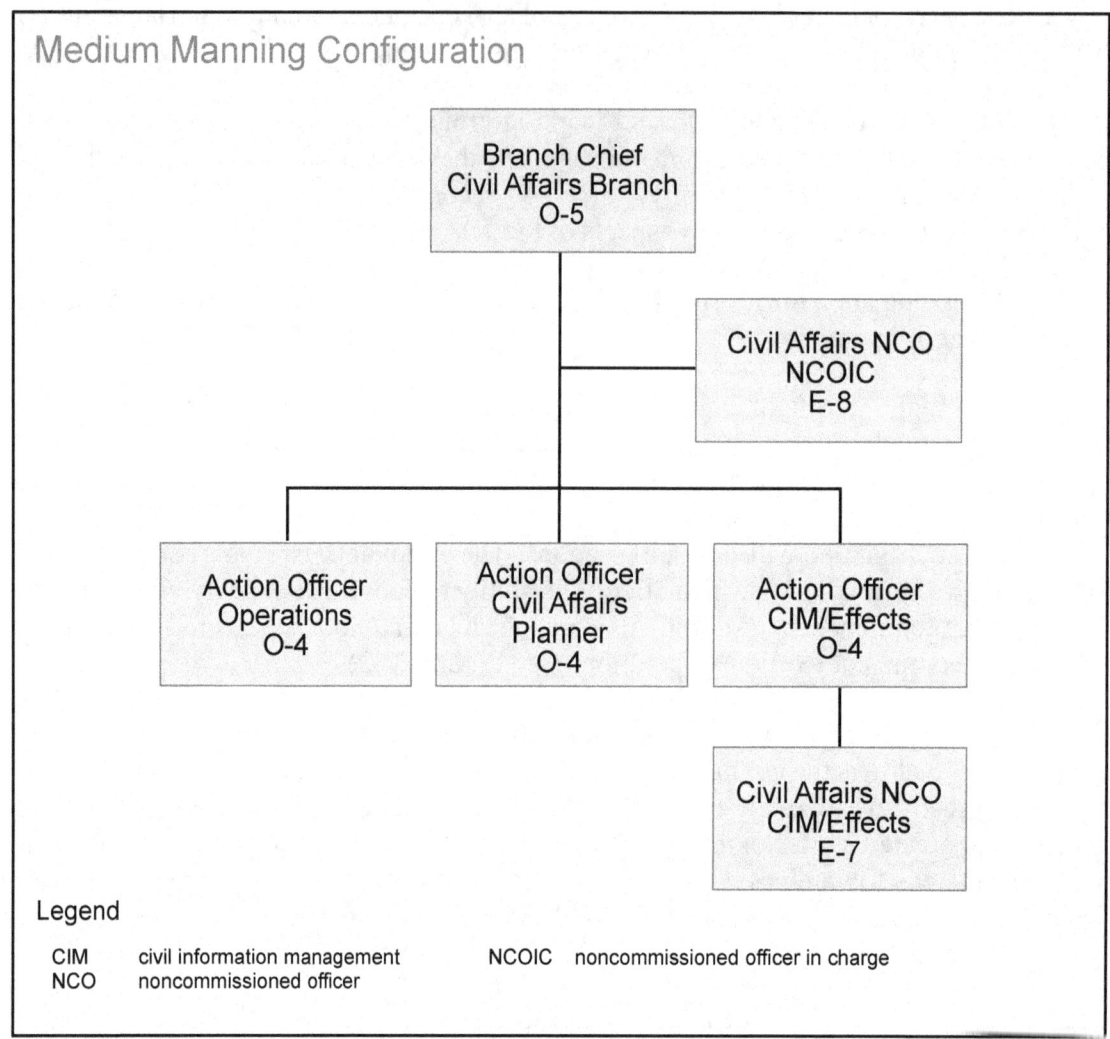

Figure IV-3. Medium Manning Configuration

(3) Heavy. The heavy, and most robust, configuration for a geographic CCMD or TSOC CA J-9 section allows the greatest flexibility and integration of CMO/CAO into broader staff analysis and functions. This configuration is best when persistent CMO/CAO planning is required for ongoing engagements and the commander needs constant assessment and awareness of the civil dimension of the AOR. This configuration enhances the commander's ability to inform policy development and strategy in regards to the civil component and application of CMO/CAO. It fully provides civil information and effects analysis in support of ongoing staff efforts and campaign plan development, and provides a robust section to coordinate multiple exercises requiring CMO/CAO and stability operations input and development (see Figure IV-4).

7. Other Civil Affairs Considerations in Support of Joint Operations

a. CA staff provide input and support to the JIPOE through analysis and synthesis of the civil environment to the intelligence directorate of a joint staff (J-2). This input complements the military intelligence efforts in analyzing the enemy threat and the OE.

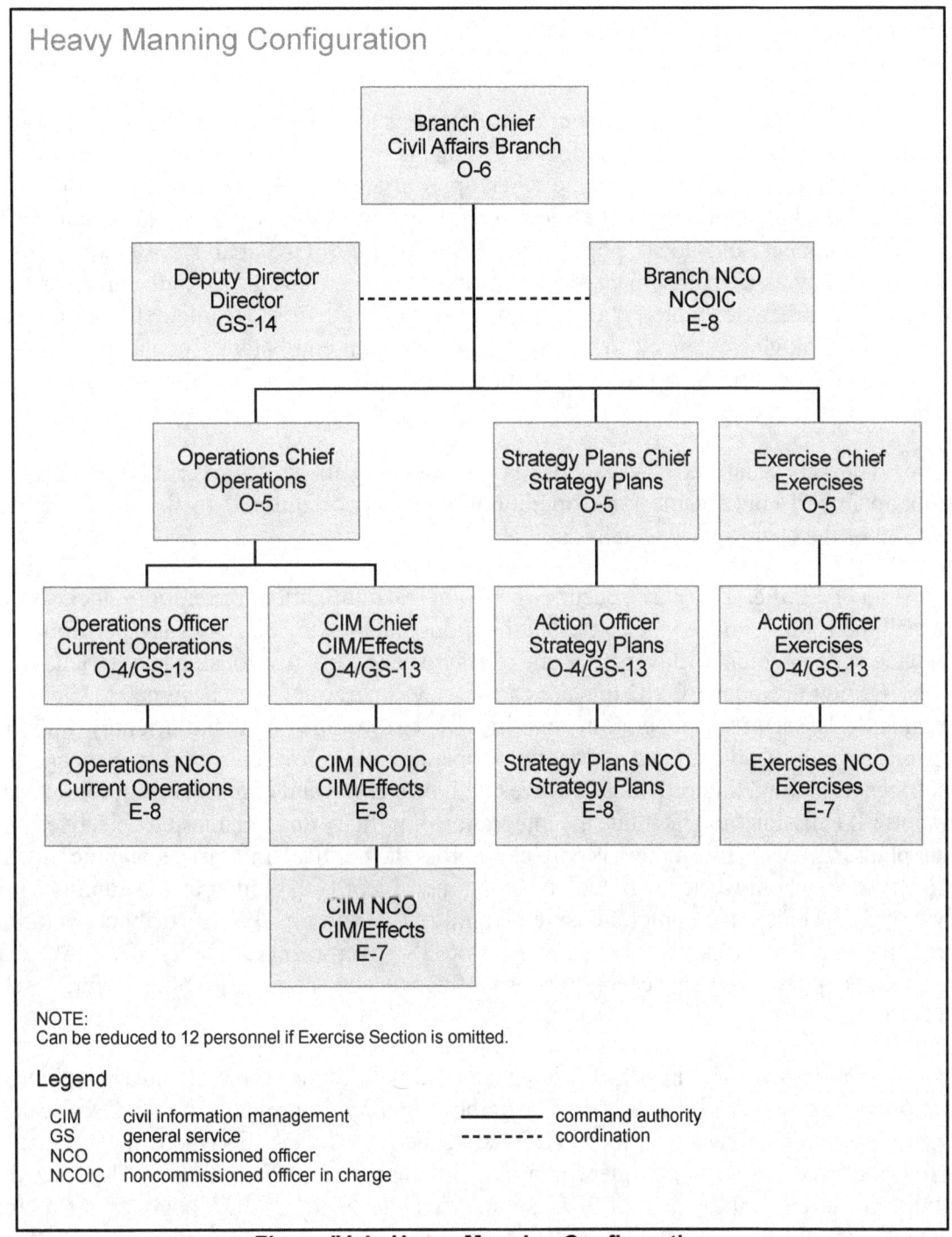

Figure IV-4. Heavy Manning Configuration

Rigorous staff efforts for developing civil understanding early in the planning process are important, and coordination with the J-2 responsible for the JIPOE is critical. CA work to provide continued analysis and engagement with key leaders, organizations (interagency or other NGOs), and population segments. CA strive to be the cultural experts for the area of operations and enhance the JIPOE with key civil and cultural considerations. The analysis of civil considerations should follow the ASCOPE framework.

See Appendix B, "Planning Considerations for Civil Affairs Operations," for more information on ASCOPE analysis.

b. CA provide civil environment considerations and analysis into the joint targeting coordination board and targeting process. CA planners provide nonlethal targeting options to support the commander's end state when appropriate and support lethal targeting with analysis of second and third order effects and mitigate the effects of lethal targeting on the civil environment and local population. Specifically, CA analysis supports target development by participating in target system analysis, electronic target folder, and target list development processes which is the responsibility of joint fires. Nonlethal targeting can include technologies designed to separate civilians from combatants (ocular interruption devices, warning munitions) as well as those intended to influence the attitudes of the population as a whole.

c. The following six-phase model is not intended to be a universally prescriptive template for all conceivable joint operations and may be tailored to the character and duration of the operation to which it applies:

(1) **Shape.** This phase occurs when joint and multinational operations, inclusive of normal and routine military activities, and various interagency activities are performed to dissuade or deter potential adversaries and to assure or solidify relationships with friends and allies. During this phase, CMO that are carried out as part of NA are designed to support a commander's security cooperation activities that develop allied and friendly military capabilities for self-defense and multinational operations, improve information exchange and intelligence sharing, and provide US forces with peacetime and contingency access. CAO support FID missions and facilitate the integration of military and US mission objectives into joint planning. Civil information is collected across the political, military, economic, social, information, and infrastructure model to build trends, identify exploitable vulnerabilities in a civil system, and enable comprehensive planning. CA participate in security cooperation through military-to-military training and increase HN government capability. The CAO goal in the shape phase is to gain access, increase influence, and share information to further US objectives.

(2) **Deter.** The intent of this phase is to deter undesirable adversary action by demonstrating the capabilities and resolve of the joint force. During this phase, CA planners coordinate with interagency partners, IGOs, and, occasionally, NGOs who work together to enable the execution of subsequent phases of the campaign. Specifically, CAO set the conditions for the employment of PRC, support the legitimacy of the HN government, and integrate the capabilities of IGO, NGO, and interagency partners that support unity of effort. CAO consider nontraditional partner capabilities in joint planning and enable partners to apply resources effectively by providing timely and accurate information. Incorporation of civil information into mission analysis identifies critical vulnerabilities in a civil system and ways to mitigate them.

(3) **Seize Initiative.** JFCs seek to seize initiative through the application of appropriate joint force capabilities such as execution of PRC measures. During this phase, CA units, in conjunction with the HN, establish conditions for stability by working through

local leaders to avoid civilian casualties and damage to property, coordinating protection plans that leverage local-national capability, and preparing for disruptions in essential services and limitations on freedom of movement by civilians. CA planners continue to refine transition planning in coordination with the JFC staff and appropriate partners.

(4) **Dominate.** This phase focuses on breaking the enemy's will for organized resistance or, in noncombat situations, control of the OE. During this phase, CAO support the denial of adversary force access to population and resources, enable proactive IO, and minimize adversary support among the local populations. Consideration of CAO during planning contributes to operational design by addressing the requirements of the civilian population in the operational area. CAO and stability tasks are conducted as needed to facilitate smooth transition between phases. Planning and coordination by CA planners continues to focus on stability and transition.

(5) **Stabilize.** CMO and the execution of CAO are likely to become the main effort during this phase, in which there may be no fully functional, legitimate civil governing authority. During this phase, CA units may be required to provide transitional military authority, integrating the efforts of multinational, interagency, IGO, or NGO partners until legitimate local entities are functioning. CA forces leverage previously collected civil information to prioritize stability tasks necessary for the speedy return to a stable state. CA may also participate in civil-military teaming to enable efforts such as reconstruction, stabilization, and reestablishing government functions and essential services. Examples of civil-military teaming include PRTs and DOS field advance civilian teams. Civil-military teams, supported by joint forces, may enter the operational area to establish or restore civil security and provide humanitarian relief.

(6) **Enable Civil Authority.** This phase is characterized by joint force support to legitimate civil governance in theater. The main effort of CA forces will most likely be SCA and providing support to the JFC and DOS in the planning and execution of CAO in accordance with titles and treaties for post-conflict operations. Upon termination of CAO, the HN or interagency partner assumes responsibility. Furthermore, CAO facilitate the transition of military authority to legitimate government authority. During this final phase, CA units will act in a supporting role to the lawful civil authority in the region and assist with the return to shaping operations.

Intentionally Blank

CHAPTER V
COORDINATION

> *"The continually changing global security environment requires increased and improved communications and coordination among the numerous agencies and organizations working to achieve national security objectives. This cooperation is best achieved through active interagency involvement, building on the core competencies and successful experiences of all."*
>
> **JP 3-08, Interorganizational Coordination During Joint Operations**

1. General

a. Interorganizational coordination is an essential requirement for unified action. The JFC and his staff should understand each interorganizational partner's roles, responsibilities, and procedures. The joint force and the country team should facilitate interorganizational coordination. The JFC, in coordination with the COM, should determine whether the CMOC can serve as the USG's primary interface for other government departments and agencies, IPI, IGOs, NGOs, and MNFs.

(1) The JFC may have considerably more planning resources than other partners. The JFC should use planning resources to achieve unified action, even when DOD is not the lead USG agency.

(2) Civil-military relationships, fostered through CMO, can enhance economic, political, and social stability. Annex V (Interagency Coordination) identifies interagency support requirements for adaptive planning. Annex V should address interagency partners. JFCs utilize annex V to incorporate the efforts and resources of interagency, IGO, and NGO communities into military operations, and vice versa.

For more details concerning annex V (Interagency Coordination), refer to CJCSM 3130.03, Adaptive Planning and Execution (APEX) Planning Formats and Guidance.

(3) In many situations, the HN and the private sector also will have major roles in coordination with the interagency partners, IGOs, and NGOs. A JFC's effective use of CMO improves the integration of the military effort and objectives with other participating organizations and their diplomatic, economic, and informational objectives, both in coordination with and on the behalf of the HN and private sector.

b. **Interorganizational Coordination at the National Levels**

(1) Military power is integrated with the other instruments of national power to advance and defend US values, interests, and objectives. To accomplish this integration, the Armed Forces interact with the other USG departments and agencies to facilitate mutual understanding of the capabilities, limitations, and consequences of military and civilian actions. They also identify the ways in which military and nonmilitary capabilities best complement each other.

(2) Regional instability is prevalent in the global environment. Interorganizational coordination can enable emerging pluralistic governments to build civil-military relations which mitigate irregular threats. Military operations must be integrated with the activities of interagency partners, as well as with MNFs, NGOs, and IGOs.

(3) Joint operational planners should consider all instruments of national power and use interagency coordination to identify which agencies best employ these instruments to achieve the national security objectives. IGOs, NGOs, and the private sector are also significant participants.

(4) Each organization brings its own culture, philosophy, goals, practices, and skills to the table, so diversity can be the strength of this process. Successful coordination and planning enables these diverse agencies and organizations with different goals to achieve unity of effort. Understanding how military efforts interface with other organizations toward USG objectives is essential for achieving unified action. Unified action includes military, national, and cultural considerations. (See Figure V-1)

For detailed discussions about interagency coordination and intergovernmental coordination, see JP 3-08, Interorganizational Coordination During Joint Operations.

c. **Procedures for Effective Cooperation**

(1) The USAID administrator usually is designated as the USG HA coordinator for emergency response. However, various agencies' different and sometimes conflicting goals, policies, procedures, and decision-making techniques make unity of effort a challenge. Some NGOs may have policies that are purposely antithetical to both the US military forces and USG departments and agencies, but they may have resources and capabilities that may promote the accomplishment of military objectives.

(2) The interagency, IGO, and NGO process often is described as "more art than science" while military operations tend to depend on structure and doctrine. However, some of the techniques, procedures, and systems of military C2 can assist in obtaining unity of effort if they are adjusted to the dynamic world of interagency, IGO, and NGO activities.

Some Considerations for Unified Action		
Military	**National**	**Cultural**
• Targeting	• National policies	• Heritage
• Fire support coordination	• Theater strategy	• Cultural resources
• Air defense	• Goals and objectives	• Language/communication
• Teamwork and trust	• Consensus building	• Media relations
• Doctrine, organization, and training	• Intergovermental relations	• Law enforcement
• Equipment	• North Atlantic Treaty Organization	• Religious factors
		• Cultural/historic property

Figure V-1. Some Considerations for United Action

Unity of effort can only be achieved through close, continuous interagency and interdepartmental coordination and cooperation, which are necessary to overcome confusion over objectives, inadequate structure or procedures, and bureaucratic and personal limitations. The Army aligns both a US Army AC CA element and a US Army Reserve CA command with each GCC (with the exception of US Northern Command). Found only in the US Army Reserve, CA commands are staffed with functional experts possessing a wide range of critical civilian skills. These functional experts are knowledgeable in working with their respective civilian counterpart agencies responsible for their functional specialty. As such, they already are experienced in the duties, responsibilities, and in some cases the agenda(s) of such agencies.

d. **Foreign Policy Advisor (FPA)**

(1) DOS assigns CCMDs an FPA who provides diplomatic considerations and enables informal linkage with embassies in the AOR and with DOS leading to greater interagency coordination.

(2) The FPA provides the GCC the following additional capabilities:

(a) Supplies information regarding DOS policy goals and objectives that are relevant to the GCC's theater strategy.

(b) Uses regional knowledge and language skills to assist the GCC in translating national objectives into military strategy.

(c) Coordinates with, and facilitates cooperation between, the primary US representatives and military personnel or their designated representatives.

(3) Under certain circumstances, an FPA may be assigned to strategic, operational, or tactical level organizations.

e. **Interagency Structure in Foreign Countries**

(1) The COM (normally an ambassador) has responsibility for all activities and authority over all elements of the USG in a country, except that authority regarding military forces assigned or attached to a CCMD. Other key USG organizations in place within most nations include the United States defense attaché office (USDAO) and the security assistance organization (called by various specific names, such as the office of defense cooperation, office of defense coordination, the security assistance office, and the military group largely governed by the preference of the receiving country)—both part of the country team. In some countries, a single military office may perform these two functions. It is important to understand the differences between these agencies when conducting theater interagency coordination.

(2) **COM.** The ambassador is the senior representative of the President in an HN and is responsible for policy decisions and the activities of USG in the country. The COM integrates the programs and resources of all USG departments and agencies represented on the country team. The COM coordinates USG responses to HN crises. Additionally, the

COM may work directly with the GCC and subordinate JFCs during crisis action planning. US forces under the GCC's command are not subject to the COM's statutory authority, but the COM's diplomatic responsibilities tie US strategic objectives to joint operations. In special cases, the COM has the authority to deny US military access into the country and can compel military personnel to leave.

(a) **US DAO.** The defense attaché (normally the senior defense official) is the COM's principal military advisor on defense and national security issues, the senior diplomatically accredited DOD military officer assigned to a US diplomatic mission, and the single point of contact for all DOD matters involving the embassy or DOD elements assigned to or working from the embassy. Service attachés also comprise the USDAO. Defense attachés liaise with their HN counterparts. The attachés also serve the ambassador and coordinate with, and represent, their respective Military Departments on Service matters. The attachés assist the security cooperation activities (e.g., FID programs) by exchanging information with the GCCs' staffs on HN military, social, economic, and political conditions.

(b) **Security Assistance Organization.** Security assistance organizations are GCCs representatives for security cooperation activities, including security assistance programs. The GCC's representatives include military assistance advisory groups, military missions and groups, offices of defense and military cooperation, liaison groups, and, in exceptional cases, defense attaché personnel designated to perform security cooperation activities.

(3) **Country Team.** The country team construct provides the foundation for rapid interagency consultation, coordination, and action on recommendations from the field and effective execution of US missions, programs, and policies. The country team typically includes political, public diplomacy (including PA), economic, administrative, and consular officers as well as a regional security and communications staff. The senior defense official and representatives from USG departments and agencies (e.g., LE and USAID) are often represented on the team. The country team is not adequately staffed to respond to various crises and may require augmentation from the interagency community.

(a) Country teams enable USG agencies to coordinate their plans and operations and keep one another and the COM informed of their activities.

(b) The GCC is not a member of the diplomatic mission but he may participate or be represented in country team meetings and coordination.

f. **Considerations for Effective Cooperation**

(1) Organizational differences between the US forces and other USG departments and agencies complicate finding an appropriate counterpart. Another significant difficulty is the determination of the primary agency for a given interagency activity. Further, overall lead authority in a contingency operation is likely to be exercised not by the GCC, but by a US ambassador or other senior civilian official, who will provide policy and goals for all USG departments and agencies and US forces.

(2) Field coordinators may not be vested to speak for parent departments, agencies, or organizations.

(3) Department and agency policies, processes, and procedures differ greatly within the interagency community. These differences may present significant challenges to interagency coordination. The various USG departments and agencies often have different, and sometimes inconsistent, goals, policies, procedures, and decision-making techniques, which make unified action a challenge. Additionally, individual agency perspectives, core values, and organizational culture can cause friction in the interagency environment. To address these problems, DOS (including USAID) and DOD have developed guidelines and policy to counter the factors that inhibit effective interagency efforts.

(4) The President or NSC designates the primary coordinating agency for operations involving extensive USG and multinational partners.

For further detail on interagency coordination at the national level, refer to JP 3-08, Interorganizational Coordination During Joint Operations.

2. Host Nation and Foreign Nation

a. CMO promote military objectives through coordination with HN and FN partners. CMO identifies resources, to include potential host-nation support (HNS) and foreign nation support (FNS). CMO can also help prevent unnecessary civilian hardship by advocating US and HN legal obligations and moral considerations.

b. The functional specialists assist HN or FN governmental organizations and agencies. In turn, this enhances joint force access to negotiate HNS or FNS.

c. A public-private partnership may be an effective way to support CMO objectives. Leveraging the private sector puts an HN face on the operations and has the potential to gain greater acceptance by the IPI. It also may reduce the need to use military assets to support civilian operations.

3. Multinational

a. US military forces should understand social and cultural considerations related to multinational operations.

b. Multinational partners' agendas and interests may differ from the US. Commanders of partner nations' forces may not have authority to make operational decisions without approval of their home country. Furthermore, national caveats (e.g., ROE) may limit commanders' operations.

c. Figure V-2 highlights some additional MNF planning factors.

d. The GCC should recognize the differences between US forces and MNFs and harmonize planning. The GCC should be sensitive to MNF positions and ensure planning is a team effort. The GCC should standardize procedures to clarify MNFs objectives.

Planning Considerations for Multinational Forces

- Force capabilities

- Command, control, and communications—will there be problems with transfer of authority?

- Logistics—will the US have to provide support and to what extent?

- Level of training

- Deployment capability—will US transportation assets be required?

- Procedures for collecting, disseminating, and sharing intelligence (information)

- Status of existing agreements—have there already been agreements established that the joint task force will be expected to support?

- National caveats (term for restrictions member nations place on the use of their forces)—what is acceptable to the participating nation?

- Cultural and historical background

- Divergent rules of engagement

- Language differences and linguist support

Figure V-2. Planning Considerations for Multinational Forces

For further details concerning operating with MNFs, refer to JP 3-16, Multinational Operations.

4. Interagency Coordination

Within the context of DOD involvement, interagency coordination is the coordination that occurs between elements of DOD and engaged USG departments and agencies for the purpose of achieving an objective. Interagency coordination forges the vital link between the US military and the other instruments of national power.

a. JFCs contribute to unity of effort by building interagency partners' situational awareness and interoperability.

b. Organizations such as the JIACG and CMOC support interorganizational coordination.

(1) The JIACG is an interagency staff group that establishes working relationships between civilian and military operational planners. JIACGs are tailored to CCDR requirements and provide collaboration with other USG departments and agencies. Members participate in deliberate and crisis action planning and provide links back to their parent civilian agencies to help synchronize JTF operations with the efforts of interagency partners.

(2) Commanders at all levels may establish a CMOC to enhance interorganizational coordination with military operations with various interagency, HN government, multinational, civilian, and NGOs. A CA command has the capabilities to provide theater-

---

level CMOC that conducts analysis of civil considerations in coordination with the JIACG. At the CA brigade level, CMOC functions may be assigned to the joint, interagency, or multinational element.

For additional details regarding interagency coordination, see JP 3-08, Interorganizational Coordination During Joint Operations.

5. Intergovernmental Organizations

a. **IGOs are created by a formal agreement (e.g., a treaty) between two or more governments on a global or regional basis for general or specialized purposes.** NATO and the Organization for Security and Cooperation in Europe are regional security organizations, while the African Union (formerly the Organization of African Unity) and the Organization of American States are general regional organizations. A new trend toward subregional organizations also is evident, particularly in Africa where, for example, the Economic Community of West African States has taken on some security functions. These organizations have defined structures, roles, and responsibilities and may be equipped with the resources and expertise to participate in complex interagency, IGO, and NGO coordination.

b. **Coordination with IGOs**

(1) **Role of IGOs.** Humanitarian relief is a fundamental responsibility for most IGOs. IGO humanitarian relief operations range from immediate response to long-term development. Organizations such as the United Nations High Commissioner for Human Rights (UNHCHR) or the World Food Program can represent IGOs during crisis.

(2) UNOCHA facilitates IGOs' humanitarian activities and provides information. UNOCHA also organizes the consolidated appeals document to present IGO views on specific crisis to the donor community.

(3) IGOs generally have specific responsibilities. For example, The World Food Program helps deliver food and determine appropriate nutrition standards. The UNHCHR provides legal protection and material support to DCs or those in refugee-like situations.

(4) IGOs and NGOs are essential to resolve and stabilize many humanitarian crises. The JFC should coordinate with IGOs and NGOs as early as possible.

(5) Isolated joint force reaction to actual or perceived humanitarian need can be counterproductive. For example, immediate humanitarian daily rations may provide a critical stopgap but they may also distort the local market and negatively affect long-term economic development. The IGO community can help resolve such dilemmas.

(6) UNOCHA often provides coordination centers. NGOs commonly utilize these centers, as will the US embassy. UNOCHA facilities transition to HN government ministries, if the government is functioning.

(7) UNOCHA headquarters in Geneva can provide information and communications links until the local UNOCHA coordination center is established in the operational area.

6. Nongovernmental Organizations

a. **Role of NGOs.** Working independently, alongside the US military, or with other USG departments and agencies, NGOs assist everywhere HA is needed. NGOs range in size and experience from those with multimillion dollar budgets and decades of global experience to newly created small organizations dedicated to a particular emergency or disaster. **Capability, equipment, resources, and expertise vary greatly from one NGO to another.** NGOs are involved in such diverse activities as education, technical projects, relief activities, DC assistance, public policy, and development programs. The sheer number of lives they affect, the resources they provide, and the moral authority conferred by their humanitarian focus enable NGOs to wield a great deal of influence within the interagency and international communities. In fact, individual organizations often are funded by national and international donor agencies as implementing partners to carry out specific functions. Similarly, internationally active NGOs may employ indigenous groups, such as the Mother Teresa Society in Kosovo, as local implementing partners.

(1) There are thousands of NGOs, which can be US, HN, or third country organizations.

(2) JFCs must verify that particular organizations are not subject to economic sanctions programs administered by the Department of the Treasury's Office of Foreign Assets Control.

b. NGOs carefully guard against the perception that their activities have been co-opted for military purposes. NGOs missions are humanitarian and not military. Commanders factor NGOs activities and capabilities into their assessment to integrate them into the selected COA without the appearance of collusion.

(1) Humanitarian organizations generally coordinate by sectors such as health and food. Joint forces should contact local NGO sector representatives to identify links to the larger NGO community. Joint forces should coordinate with humanitarian organizations in the most open forum possible (i.e., outside the wire).

(2) NGOs very often lack robust logistic capability and transportation assets, and may ask for joint force support.

c. Private organizations sometimes voluntarily share information about local and regional affairs and civilian attitudes. Collegial relations can enhance such disclosures. Virtually all IGO and NGO operations interact with military operations in some way—they use the same (normally limited) lines of communications; they draw on the same sources for local interpreters and translators; and they compete for buildings and storage space. CMO enables operational information to be shared between joint forces, IGOs, and NGOs.

(1) Information acquired through interaction with IGOs and NGOs can be invaluable in answering CCIRs. Personnel conducting CMO should submit reports that answer CCIRs through appropriate channels. However, this information and knowledge should be acquired in a collateral fashion, and not part of intelligence collection operations. NGOs may share what they know of the environment within a CMOC, but they will not likely cooperate with active intelligence gathering.

(2) Conversely, NGOs expect US forces to provide information such as mine locations and hostile areas.

7. The Private Sector

The private sector is an umbrella term that may be applied in the United States and in foreign countries to any or all of the nonpublic or commercial individuals and businesses, specified nonprofit organizations, most of academia and other scholastic institutions, and selected NGOs. The private sector can assist the USG by sharing information, identifying risks, performing vulnerability assessments, assisting in contingency and crisis action planning, and providing other assistance as appropriate.

a. **Role of Private Sector.** The NSC coordinates joint operations with other instruments of national power. The private sector plays a significant role in the US economic and informational instruments. Leveraging the private sector, during phase 0, IV, and V operations, to assume such roles as economic and business development, is often the most expedient, effective, and enduring way to achieve a political end state built on broad-based, long-term US interests. Joint forces and interagency partners should incorporate private sector perspectives in plans and strategy. CMO encourage individual businesses, trade associations, and other private sector organizations to foster dialogue with the US military and the HN government. **The sharing of operational information with and coordinating support of the private sector is an essential element of successful CMO.**

b. Communication between the US military and the private sector promotes US interests, policy, and objectives. CMO, through establishing and maintaining communications is one of the best ways to unify military and public/private partnerships and best practices to improve the FN's or HN's internal security and promote stability operations in the operational area. Stability operations tasks, when dealing with the private sector, includes fostering dialogue, helping revive the interface between all parties, including encouraging citizen-driven, bottom-up economic activity, and constructing necessary infrastructure. HN and regional private sector institutions often possess skills and expertise to contribute to the overall US objectives.

c. Partnerships between the public and private sectors to protect critical infrastructure are often essential. The private sector can own and operate a large portion of the HN's or FN's critical infrastructure; government agencies have access to critical threat information, and each controls security programs, research and development, and other resources that may be more effective if shared.

d. The lead agency for USG response to disasters or emergencies overseas is DOS, specifically OFDA, which typically works through or with the HN or an IGO to coordinate with the private sector. DOD normally supports DOS through FHA or FCM.

APPENDIX A
SERVICE CAPABILITIES

The purpose of this appendix is to provide an overview of some of the Service capabilities that would most likely support CMO. Each annex to this appendix will discuss a different Service capability.

Intentionally Blank Page

ANNEX A TO APPENDIX A
CIVIL AFFAIRS SERVICE CAPABILITIES

1. United States Army

The Global Force Management Implementation Guidance and Forces for Unified Commands Memorandum are the documents that assign CA units to the respective CCDRs for periods of other than war or contingencies.

a. **Regular Army.** Provides two CA brigades: one that is designed to support SOF operations, and one that is designed to support CF. CA battalions with a headquarters and headquarters company (HHC) are flexible, multipurpose organizations for training, equipping, and deploying CA companies and teams. The CA battalion directly supports commanders on forward deployed C2 nodes with planners and facilitators for CAO and theater security cooperation and contingency operations at the strategic and operational level. The CA companies directly support brigade combat teams (BCTs), special operations task forces, theater security cooperation, and contingency operations at the operational and tactical level. CATs are four man elements that provide the GCC with a direct link to the civilian population and HN military forces on the ground. Additionally, a CMSE can be formed by adding a two person planning element to a CAT to support specific operations.

(1) USSOCOM provides regionally focused CA forces structured to deploy rapidly and provide initial CA support to SOF and contingency operations.

(2) Joint Staff J-3 provides the CF CA force that is similar to the SOF CA forces and designed to support the CF principally through the Army Service component commands (ASCCs).

(3) CA Brigade (Airborne) (Special Operations). The USASOC CA brigade consists of an HHC and five regionally focused battalions structured to deploy rapidly and provide initial CA support to SOF and contingency operations. The CA brigade has a worldwide mission and provides US SOF with a responsive, flexible, and modular CA force package. The brigade has the ability to deploy classified and unclassified communications links that provide communications capability with supported forces (SOF and conventional), IPI, IGOs, interagency partners, private sector and NGOs. The brigade has the structure to form the core of the theater-level JCMOTF and is C2 system-capable.

(a) The CA battalions are flexible, multipurpose organizations for training, equipping, and deploying task organized CATs in support of CMO. They provide CA support to the respective geographic combatant command, as necessary by attaching task organized elements from their headquarters or attached CA assets. These CA elements support SOF at the operational and tactical levels. The CA battalion has an HHC, a CAPT, and a CMOC including a CLT and CIM cell.

(b) Each CA battalion has five organic CA line companies, each with a CMOC. Each CA line company can provide C2 to the assigned CATs and can provide planning, coordination, and assessment at the tactical level.

(4) CA Brigade (Conventional Force Support). The CA brigade functions as an operating force unit designated as theater available in the global forces pool assigned to FORSCOM. The CA brigade is designed as an expeditionary, operational-level CA capability that supports the Army corps or an equivalent JTF headquarters. The CA brigade possesses a special functions cell and a PA staff capability. Its mission focus is development, reconstruction, and stabilization. The CA brigade enables SCA and possesses the operational C2 structure to form a JCMOTF. The brigade headquarters provide C2 and staff supervision of the operations of the CA brigade and assigned CA battalions or attached units. The CA brigade plans, enables, shapes, and manages CAO with and through IPI, IGOs, NGOs, and other government departments and agencies by means of its CLTs and CMOC.

(a) CA brigade consists of an HHC and five regionally focused battalions structured to deploy rapidly and provide CA support to CF across the range of military operations.

(b) The five battalions with their organic companies have the capability to plan, enable, shape, and manage CAO; provide dedicated support to stability operations; and enable, enhance, and support CMO missions assigned to the theater Army command by the TCP. The battalion provides tactical-level CA support to a division command or an equivalent-level Army command/JTF during stability operations.

(c) The CA battalion has an HHC, a CAPT, and a CMOC including a CLT O&I and CIM cell. Each CA battalion has five organic CA line companies, each with a CMOC. Each CA line company can provide C2 to the assigned CATs and can provide planning, coordination, and assessment at the tactical level in support of BCTs or other units.

b. **United States Army Reserve (USAR).** The majority of the Army's CA organizations are USAR and consist of commands, brigades, battalions, and companies capable of supporting SOF and CF at the tactical, operational, and strategic levels

(1) There are currently four CA commands, each commanded by a USAR brigadier general. They are regionally aligned to support United States Pacific Command, United States European Command/United States Africa Command, United States Central Command, and United States Southern Command. The CA command develops plans, policy, and programs through planning teams, fusion of IM, engagement, and analysis at the strategic and theater level. Its primary mission is to provide theater-level CA planning, coordination, policies, and programs in support of stabilization, reconstruction, and development efforts. The CA command may deploy a theater-level CMOC to coordinate, analyze, and enable policies, programs, and CMO capabilities in support of the GCC and to develop and manage the strategic-level civil inputs to the COP for the GCC. A typical CA command consists of an HHC, five CAPTs, and a CMOC capable of split operations (forward and rear) with three functional specialty cells, two CLTs, O&I, and one CIM cell. Each CA command has one or more CA brigades assigned; each CA brigade has two or more subordinate CA battalions. All are regionally focused and have expertise in the cultural and political aspects of countries within a region.

(2) CA brigades function as the regionally focused, expeditionary, operational level CA capability that supports an ASCC/corps or JTF. Dependent on the staffing, the brigade commander may be required to be dual-hatted: commander and staffer. Without a CA element on the staff, the commander may serve as the ASCC/corps/JTF commander's senior CA advisor. The brigade's focus is development, reconstruction, and stabilization. The CA brigade enables SCA and is the operational C2 system structure to form a JCMOTF, if required. The brigade headquarters provide C2 and staff supervision of the operations of the CA brigade and assigned CA battalions or attached units. Its focus is on tactical and operational employment of CA forces and attached CMO forces. The CA brigade plans, enables, shapes, and manages CAO in coordination with IPI, IGOs, NGOs, and the other government departments and agencies through its CLT, which is found in the CA brigades CMOC.

(3) The CA battalion focus is on the division commander's ready-capability to plan, enable, shape, and manage stabilization and reconstruction and the enablement/reestablishment/support of civil administration at the provincial level. USAR CA battalions possess CA functional specialty support in the areas of rule of law, governance, public health and welfare, and infrastructure, and provide tactical CA support to the division command. This battalion has an HHC, a CAPT, a CMOC capable of providing one CLT, a functional specialty cell, and four CA companies, each with a CMOC and five CATs. Each CA line company can provide planning, coordination, and assessment at the tactical level, and C2 to the assigned CATs. CA companies are normally in direct support of either BCTs or maneuver enhancement brigades.

(4) **Employment Considerations.** Reserve CA employment as attached forces requires detailed management of time-phased force and deployment data and task organizations by unit identification code. Supported unit commanders are responsible to provide the vast majority of administrative and logistic support because these capabilities are not usually organic to CA. By table of organization and equipment, CA units are authorized the latest in conventional and special operations communications equipment and computers to allow secured and unsecured Internet communication, over-the-horizon and satellite capable radios and laptop computers with access to the Internet. Additionally, CA units must be equipped with the current and most common civilian communications equipment to allow them to interface with IGOs, NGOs, IPI, and private sector in the operational area. Specific requirements beyond these capabilities are determined during mission analysis and forwarded to the supported command as a statement of requirements.

2. **United States Marine Corps**

a. The United States Marine Corps (USMC) has the capability to plan and conduct CMO across the range of military operations. A dedicated CA structure is maintained within the RC and AC, consisting of three RC civil affairs groups (CAGs) (with a fourth being activated in fiscal year 2014), each commanded by a colonel (O-6) and three Marine expeditionary force (MEF) CA detachments, each lead by a major (O-4). The CA detachments are organic to the MEF, they augment and reinforce the capabilities of the MEF or other major subordinate elements of the Marine air-ground task force (MAGTF). Should the AC CA detachments be unavailable or insufficient in size for the task at hand, MAGTF commanders may request additional support from a CAG via their Marine Corps component commander. CAGs are mobilized when a MEF is provided to a CCMD for planning or operations. Each CAG is regionally oriented to the projected employment of the MEF it supports. In addition to supporting major combat operations, USMC CA forces participate in security cooperation efforts when made available by their component commanders.

b. USMC CMO typically are centrally planned by the MAGTF staff for decentralized execution by assigned forces. Each MAGTF has organic air, ground, C2, and logistic capabilities that provide immediate and integrated CMO options to the JFC. Operational maneuver from the sea, implementing ship-to-objective maneuver and seabased logistics, enables rapid execution of USMC CMO, without the need to establish extensive infrastructure ashore. Each MEF's assigned AC CA detachment will provide initial CA support to a deployed MAGTF. Qualified Marines from each MEF's aligned CAG are prepared to deploy within days of a validated request, even if no Presidential Reserve Call-up is authorized. Additional volunteers may provide further support, by Presidential Reserve Call-up of CAG elements for contingencies, or by mobilization of entire CAGs. Regardless of size, USMC CA elements will require support from the MAGTF in such areas as transportation, health support, supply, and messing.

c. USMC CMO are performed to directly support the MAGTF's assigned mission, which typically is of limited duration, performed under austere conditions, and expeditionary in nature. These missions might include NEOs, the offload of maritime pre-positioning ships, FHA in response to complex emergencies, amphibious operations, or employment as an enabler for follow-on operations. These types of limited contingency operations rarely will allow for exhaustive coordination of details or extensive planning prior to execution. Instead, the MAGTF must understand the goals and priorities of the JFCs, COMs, and US embassy country teams within the operational area. CA and CMO initially focus on confirming, updating, and disseminating the assessment of the situation; providing an initial response to emergencies; stabilizing the operational area; and enhancing the legitimacy of the force. Initial CA plans prepare for a transition of responsibilities to other agencies, such as other US military forces, interagency partners, IGOs, or NGOs. USMC CA are also prepared to assist a supported Navy commander. This support might be required when amphibious shipping is tasked to transship evacuees, provide emergency medical support to civilian casualties, or control sea approaches, pier space, or cargo handling.

d. As a self-contained, combined arms force, the MAGTF may become involved in sustained operations ashore. These situations will require detailed coordination with the GCC's CA assets, IGOs, NGOs, multinational partners, and the other interagency organizations operating within the MAGTF's area of operations. Deployed CA forces (and those accessed via reachback) facilitate mission accomplishment by focusing on civil considerations. They leverage the MAGTF's resources, especially its logistical capability, by integrating the complementary capabilities of other agencies to achieve success and allow timely force redeployment. Throughout, Marine CMO efforts help the commander to meet legal obligations and moral considerations while accomplishing the military mission.

3. United States Navy

All United States Navy (USN) maritime CA units are based in the continental United States (CONUS) and report administratively to the Chief of Naval Operations via Commander, US Fleet Forces Command and Commander, Navy Expeditionary Combat Command (NECC), a subordinate organization of US Fleet Forces Command.

a. Navy CA forces support naval units engaged in the conduct of CMO within the maritime domain. Among the many capabilities found within NECC are coastal riverine force, explosives ordnance disposal, naval construction force (NCF), expeditionary logistics support group, expeditionary security force, and the MCAST Command. MCAST Command, together with other NECC expeditionary forces or other USN forces, provides capabilities for the conduct of CMO within the coastal riverine, and near shore environments. These capabilities range from projection of CMO forces ashore from aircraft carrier and amphibious warfare ships utilizing small surface craft and helicopters to ground transportation, engineer, communications, medical, and security force capabilities provided by NECC as an adaptive force package or that are organic to individual ships. The MCAST Command serves as the link between USN forces and the civil element within the maritime domain. MCAST Command conducts CAO across the maritime domain supporting GCC, USN component commanders, numbered fleets, and strike groups, in the planning and conduct of the full range of CMO.

b. The MCAST Command is a multi-composition organization containing a mix of AC and RC. It is organized with a group headquarters staff and a functional specialty team, two regionally aligned maritime CA squadrons along with subordinate maritime CA unit headquarters and maritime civil affairs teams (MCATs). The MCAST Command is immediately available for contingency operations and is trained for worldwide operations within the maritime domain. MCAST Command core competencies include:

(1) **Maritime CA Plans and Operations.** MCAST Command provides a highly mobile group or squadron forward headquarters serving as a CMO plans and operations element integrating with Navy component and fleet headquarters that are also capable of integrating as joint CMO planners and operations staff within a JTF. This forward headquarters element is capable of providing C2 for direction of employed MCAT assessment operations and in directing/synchronizing the efforts of the CMOC. This forward headquarters maintain communications with their parent maritime CA headquarters and reachback to maritime CA functional experts.

(2) **MCAT.** MCAST Command provides regionally aligned, highly mobile MCATs capable of rapid deployment to their assigned theaters. MCATs provide a reconnaissance capability producing a civil assessment of the supported commander's area of operations. They deploy with ground and maritime mobility packages along with a robust communications suite with long-distance radio and satellite communications, digital photo and video capabilities.

(3) **CMOC.** MCAST Command is capable of establishing and operating a CMOC.

(4) **Maritime Functional Area Expertise.** MCAST Command provides a full range of functional expertise tailored for use within the maritime domain. Additionally, MCAST Command provides unique functional expertise in marine fisheries and resources, commercial port operations, and harbor and channel construction and maintenance.

c. **Employment Considerations.** Although MCAST Command possesses the capability to respond rapidly in support of contingency operations, its multi-composition (Active/Reserve) nature and size constrains its ability to respond to large scale operations outside of its intended purpose, the support of theater naval component forces. MCAST Command forces are not substitutes for USA or USMC CA forces and should only support other Services in extreme situations.

4. **United States Air Force**

a. The United States Air Force (USAF) does not maintain CA units. Many Air National Guard (ANG), active duty Air Force, and Air Force reserve judge advocates and paralegals are trained in CA issues and have been involved in significant CMO (e.g., PRTs in Afghanistan). A variety of functional organizations and capabilities within the Air Force Reserve Command and ANG as well as the active force can support or complement CMO. These include legal, air mobility, chaplain, health support, security forces, intelligence, surveillance, reconnaissance, civil engineering, communications, bioenvironmental, and meteorological services. In supporting CCDRs, the USAF upon request can provide specially qualified personnel for service in Army or joint CA units as specialists.

b. **ANG Readiness Center.** Access to ANG personnel with CA-related skills may be accomplished through the ANG Readiness Center, an active Air Force unit that exercises administrative control over such personnel ordered to active duty under conditions short of full mobilization.

c. The Air Force International Health Specialist (IHS) Program develops a cadre of multi-corps health professionals with expertise in CMO including domestic and international coordination. IHS personnel are ideally suited to integrate public health and welfare with all CA functional specialty areas.

5. **United States Coast Guard**

a. The United States Coast Guard (USCG) does not maintain CA. However, the Coast Guard can provide a variety of capabilities, assistance, equipment, and training in helping a country organize and establish a coast guard. USCG forces have 11 statutory missions: marine safety; search and rescue; aids to navigation; living marine resources (fisheries LE); marine environmental protection; ice operations; ports, waterways and coastal security; drug interdiction; migrant interdiction; defense readiness; and other LE.

b. The Coast Guard Model Maritime Service Code is a valuable reference for other nations to use for establishing a maritime force.

ANNEX B TO APPENDIX A
ENGINEERING

1. United States Army

a. USA has a wide variety of engineer units at division, corps, and theater level that provide particular technical capabilities required to accomplish essential, diversified tasks throughout the depth of the theater. The engineer architecture forms these units into an organization that is responsive to commanders at all echelons.

b. US Army operational engineer headquarters, assigned to Army and joint organizations, include two theater engineer commands (TECs), engineer brigades, engineer battalions, and one prime power engineer battalion. The TEC develops plans, procedures, and programs for engineer support for the theater army. The TEC commander exercises command over those engineer (or other) units (Army and joint) task-organized to the TEC, to include commercial contract construction capability such as the (USACE), NAVFAC, Air Force Civil Engineer Center, multinational, HN, or others as assigned. The TEC also may support joint and multinational commands and other elements according to lead Service responsibilities, as directed by the supported JFC. The engineer brigade, one of the Army's functional brigades, can control up to five mission-tailored engineer battalions having capabilities from any of the three engineer disciplines (combat, general, and geospatial). The engineer brigade can support a JTF or a Service or functional component command (land, air, or maritime) and provide C2 of all Service engineers and oversight of contracted engineering within an operational area. The engineer battalion can conduct engineer missions and control up to five mission-tailored engineer companies. The engineer battalion is typically found in the engineer brigade, in the maneuver enhancement brigade, or supporting a BCT. Engineer companies include a variety of combat engineer units to support the mobility, countermobility, and survivability of maneuver forces; geospatial units; and vertical and horizontal construction companies for GE. Engineer teams include specialized units for diving, mine dog detection, facilities management, construction management, geospatial planning, explosive hazards coordination, water well drilling, real estate management, quarrying, asphalt, and firefighting.

c. USACE is the Army's direct reporting unit assigned responsibility to execute Army and DOD military construction, real estate acquisition, and development of the nation's infrastructure through the civil works program. Other services include wetlands and waterway management and disaster relief support operations. With its subordinate divisions, districts, laboratories, and centers, USACE provides a broad range of engineering service support to the Military Departments, USG departments and agencies, state governments, and local authorities. The USACE also provides technical assistance and contract support to joint forces deployed worldwide.

d. US Army engineers are capable of providing the senior engineer command headquarters in the operational area or integrating into a joint force and supporting other Services as well as multinational and civilian organizations.

For additional information on the employment of USA engineers, refer to Field Manual (FM) 3-34, Engineer Operations, *and JP 3-34,* Joint Engineer Operations.

2. United States Marine Corps

a. The Marine Corps provides operating forces to conduct expeditionary operations, and its organic engineering expertise rests in expeditionary engineering. Expeditionary engineering is the organic engineering capabilities conducted to meet the maneuver, FP, and basic logistic requirements of the MAGTF. Expeditionary engineering ensures the MAGTF can operate in austere environments with organic capabilities typically for 0-6 months with limited external support to maintain operations. Expeditionary engineering provides freedom of maneuver through the application of capabilities to emplace and breach obstacles/barriers as well as build and maintain combat roads/trails, assault gap crossing, and landing zones (formerly mobility and countermobility). FP requirements are supported by mitigating the effects of adversary weapons through position hardening and emplacing barriers that support stand-off (formerly survivability). Expeditionary engineering support to enabling basic logistic requirements of the MAGTF includes limited horizontal/vertical construction, power generation and distribution, bulk liquids storage, and a working understanding of infrastructure systems to adapt them for MAGTF use (formerly GE).

b. The MEF is supported by an engineer support battalion (ESB) that is organic to the Marine logistics group (MLG) contained within the MEF. The ESB is structured to facilitate task organization and provide expeditionary engineering to the MEF. The ESB is organized to plan, coordinate, and supervise expeditionary engineering support functions. The expeditionary engineering support includes enhancing the MEF's maneuver, FP, and basic logistics. The ESB additionally provides explosive ordnance disposal (EOD) operations to the MEF.

(1) ESB provides vertical and horizontal construction, gap crossing, water purification, and mobile electric power.

(2) ESB can conduct limited counter obstacle missions.

(3) ESB is the primary USMC engineering unit to support CMO.

c. The Marine division is supported by one combat engineer battalion (CEB) which provides expeditionary engineering support through task-organized combat engineer elements. The mission of the CEB is to enhance the maneuver, FP, and basic logistic capability of the Marine division. The Marine division contains three infantry regiments, and a combat engineer company normally supports each regiment. The CEB enhances the movement of the division's operational forces in much the same manner as the ESB.

d. The Marine aircraft wing has expeditionary engineer capabilities embedded in the Marine wing support squadrons (MWSSs). These support squadrons possess an engineer company with capabilities for the construction and maintenance of expeditionary airfields, fuel handling, materials handling, and limited vertical and horizontal construction. They also can provide mobile electric power and can purify water to potable standards. Each

MWSS provides EOD support to expeditionary airfield operations. Expeditionary engineer requirements exceeding MWSS capabilities are augmented by the ESB.

e. The Marine division, wing, and MLG structure outlined here is identical for I and II MEF. The organizational structure for engineering support for III MEF is similar but slightly reduced due to smaller end strength. GE support to augment the organic MAGTF expeditionary engineering capability is provided by the First Naval Construction Division (1 NCD).

For additional information on naval construction augmentation to the Marine Corps, see Marine Corps Warfighting Publication (MCWP) 4-11.5/Navy Tactics, Techniques, and Procedures (NTTP) 4-04.1M, Seabee Operations in the MAGTF.

3. United States Navy

a. Navy civil engineering forces are organized and equipped to meet the requirements of diverse CMO engineering tasks. They are versatile, flexible, expandable, rapidly deployable, sustainable, and are able to reconstitute for expeditionary operations. Navy civil engineering forces combine the complementary but distinct capabilities of the construction and engineering operating forces of the NECC and naval amphibious construction battalions (PHIBCBs) of the naval beach groups (NBGs), the business enterprise of NAVFAC, and CCMD staff engineer positions.

(1) Because of integral working relationships, naval civil engineering forces are able to leverage a wide range and scope of engineering and construction capabilities to support the warfighter. Mission support areas include construction of advanced bases, horizontal and vertical construction, battle damage repair, the full range of facility planning, design, construction, contracting, operation and maintenance, and environmental compliance.

(2) Their expertise includes amphibious and underwater construction, construction contracting, facilities management, real estate acquisition, environmental compliance, ship-to-shore support, pier construction and repair, well-drilling, fleet hospital erection, construction of standard and nonstandard bridges, water and fuel storage and distribution, electrical power generation systems, and utilities systems. They also provide technical engineering and contract support.

b. The NCF provides the JFC with flexible expeditionary engineering forces capable of supporting a wide range of missions. The NCF primarily supports the MAGTF and Navy ashore forces as directed by existing plans and orders. The NCF also supports component missions specified by the CCDRs. NCF capabilities enable the JFC to optimize the effectiveness of dedicated Armed Forces across the range of military operations.

For more information on the missions, capabilities, and organization of the NCF refer to Navy Technical Reference Publication 4-04.2.1, Doctrinal Reference for the Naval Construction Force.

(1) NCF units enhance the MAGTF through complementary, not duplicative, support.

(2) NCF units are highly skilled specialists capable of executing projects of a more sophisticated and permanent nature than normally accomplished by USMC engineer battalions. Their capabilities include the following:

(a) Military construction engineering support to CCMDs, the USN, and the USMC.

(b) Battle damage repair.

(c) Construct and maintain expeditionary airfields, main supply routes, advanced bases and port facilities, ammunition supply points, deliberate bridging, as well as a wide range of other combat support and combat service support facilities.

(d) In a contingency environment, provide organic capability for defensive military operations and sustainment for independent operations.

(e) In a peacetime environment, provide Navy component commanders (NCCs) and joint force maritime component commanders (JFMCCs) with contributory support and GCCs with recovery operations, FHA, HCA, and other operational support with a rapid, expeditionary engineering response capability.

c. NECC provides forces to fulfill operational requirements of a CCDR exercising C2 over subordinate naval construction groups consisting of an operational naval construction regiment (NCR) and Seabee readiness group. It may deploy when two or more subordinate NCR units (e.g., five or more naval mobile construction battalions [NMCBs]) deploy to a theater. NECC is comprised of two active and three reserve NCRs, six active and six reserve NMCBs, two active construction battalion maintenance unit (CBMU) with reserve augment support, and two active underwater construction teams (UCTs). NCF units include the following:

(1) The NMCB is the NCF's main unit of action and most capable construction battalion (Seabee) unit for conducting construction and engineer operations. It is a modular task organization of air transportable, ground, and logistics elements. NMCBs can deploy rapidly as part of amphibious ready forces, maritime pre-positioning forces, and air contingency forces. It constructs advanced base facilities in support of the USN, USMC, and other Armed Forces and provides repair, maintenance, and construction support during contingency, emergency, or recovery operations.

(2) The CBMU provides follow-on public works operations, maintenance and repair at existing advanced base shore facilities or facilities constructed by NMCBs in contingency operations. It also provides public works support for various Navy expeditionary medical treatment facility configurations during military operations. Designated personnel are assigned in accordance with NTTP 4-02.4, *Expeditionary Medical Facilities*. In peacetime, CBMUs provide repair and maintenance support to US shore installations and have a secondary mission to conduct disaster recovery missions.

(3) The UCT provides underwater engineering, construction, repair, and inspection support and performs complex inshore and deep ocean underwater construction tasks, including ocean bottom surveys for potential underwater facilities.

(4) The NCR exercises C2 over subordinate NCF or other attached expeditionary units, providing planning, coordination, and oversight. It deploys when two or more subordinate NCF units deploy to a theater.

For additional information on the employment of the NCF, refer to Navy Warfare Publication (NWP) 4-04, Navy Civil Engineering Operations, and NTTP 4-04.1, Seabee Operations in the MAGTF.

d. NAVFAC is the Navy's global shore facilities manager. This command's primary mission is to provide facilities engineering, acquisition, and technical support to the operating forces of the USN and USMC. It provides construction supplemental and contingency contracting capability for planning, designing, and executing construction in theater including architectural/engineering services, real estate, environmental compliance, and base operation support/facility services. It also provides technical support across a broad spectrum of engineering and scientific disciplines during contingency and crisis action planning, and solves challenging problems related to engineering, infrastructure, and environmental compliance during contingency operations using reachback capabilities. NAVFAC also maintains standing contingency contracts with large international and continental US civil construction, engineering, and facility support service firms for contingency response missions.

For additional information on the employment of NAVFAC, refer to NWP 4-04, Navy Civil Engineering Operations.

e. PHIBCBs are an integral part of Navy civil engineering operating forces organized under the NBG. They provide over-the-shore logistic movement and construction support to amphibious forces.

For information on the employment of the PHIBCBs, refer to NWP 3-02.1, Ship to Shore Movement, and NTTP 3-02.14 (Rev A), The Naval Beach Group.

4. **United States Air Force**

a. The USAF engineering mission is to provide the necessary assets and skilled personnel to prepare and sustain global installations as stationary platforms for projecting air and space power across the range of military operations. Air operations are highly dependent on operating bases; consequently, engineering planners must participate in all stages of operational planning for bases to be available when they are needed. Air Force engineering units can deploy either as a part of an expeditionary force, or as detached units operating in support of specific missions and operational taskings. The USAF civil engineering mission in support of a typical plan or order includes airfield damage repair (ADR); emergency war damage repair to other essential facilities; force beddown; operations and maintenance; crash rescue and fire suppression; EOD; chemical, biological, radiological, and nuclear (CBRN) hazard mitigation including toxic industrial materials (TIMs); and improvised explosive devices; and construction management of emergency repair of war damage and force beddown that are necessary for employing USAF forces and weapons systems. These engineering forces are organized either as Prime Base Engineer Emergency Force (Prime BEEF), or Rapid Engineer Deployable Heavy Operational Repair Squadron, Engineer (RED HORSE) units. During any type of military operation, engineer requirements will be numerous, and military engineers may be stretched beyond their capability. A force multiplier for USAF engineering is the Air Force contract augmentation program (AFCAP) that allows civil engineers to focus on the most critical missions.

b. Prime BEEF is the primary organizational structure for supporting both mobility and in-place contingency requirements. The principle objective of deploying Prime BEEF teams is to beddown and support an air and space expeditionary task force. Force beddown generally divides into three categories—aircraft, personnel, and infrastructure support. Aircraft support provides the maintenance shops, hangars, squadron operations centers, munitions storage, fuel storage, and other facilities directly supporting the flying mission. Personnel support provides the housing, feeding facilities, latrines, showers, administrative offices, and other indirect support facilities. Infrastructure support provides the utility systems, solid and hazardous waste disposal, roads, and communications that serve the beddown site. Beddown locations range from main operating bases with adequate existing facilities to bare bases with no facilities other than runways, taxiways, and aircraft parking aprons. Tasks accomplished by Prime BEEF units include airfield support, fire protection, fuel systems setup and support, EOD functions, construction of FP infrastructure, base defense, base denial, ADR, facility repair, and utility repair.

c. The AFCAP provides commanders with another option to relieve military engineers, particularly for critical high threat or critical missions. AFCAP has installation support capabilities that mirror the USAF engineering and force support sustainment services functional capabilities. AFCAP can provide all the installation support services and operations inherent in the Air Force engineering and force support sustainment services functional areas, except EOD; CBRN operations; and field operations and mortuary affairs. AFCAP may be used after an initial military beddown response, for facility erection and construction requirements, or to support recovery operations at existing locations across the full spectrum of conflicts.

d. RED HORSE squadrons and their associated unit type code configurations provide highly mobile, largely self-sufficient, rapidly deployable echelons to support major construction requirements and to repair heavy war damage. RED HORSE units are stand-alone squadrons not tied to peacetime base support. They provide Air Force component commanders a dedicated and flexible airfield with base heavy construction and repair capability. This capability allows the GCCs to react, initiate movement, and support missions as the air order of battle dictates. RED HORSE units often accomplish major construction in forward locations, in advance of the main deploying force. They provide heavy horizontal (earth moving and pavements) and vertical (facility and utility skills such as petroleum, oils, and lubricants; structural, mechanical, and power generation) engineer capability, and possess special capabilities such as quarry operation (blasting and rock crushing), well drilling, concrete or asphalt batch plant operations, specialized building construction (K-Spans), and constructive explosive operations. RED HORSE units also are required to be current in a variety of other capabilities across the range of military operations.

For more details on engineering, refer to JP 3-34, Joint Engineer Operations.

ANNEX C TO APPENDIX A
MEDICAL CIVIL-MILITARY OPERATIONS

1. Overview

An assessment of total health support requirements for CMO comes from careful mission analysis, resource application, and an adequate survey of existing medical care infrastructure. This assessment should then be coordinated within the theater health support community. Medical civil-military operations (MCMO) will be performed by health support units directly and in conjunction with CA units. These activities must always be in line with the overall JFC's CMO objectives. DODI 2205.02, *Humanitarian and Civic Assistance (HCA) Activities*, lists medical and other health interventions as primary tools to promote the security interests of the USG and the HN, enhance operational readiness skills of US military units, and promote USG foreign policy interests. There is significant DOD policy on HCA and HA based on legal authority within Title 10, USC. Additionally, there are several funding sources for CA and medical forces to perform MCMO missions legally and effectively.

2. Civil Affairs and the Health Sector

a. It is important for public health/medical personnel to be involved directly with the assessments, planning, and execution of CMO that directly and indirectly affect the health sector. The health sector is a term used internationally to include all aspects within a country or area that affects the population's health. It is critical to consider all the aspects of that particular country to develop positive relationships and acquire information to maximize the health of the largest number of people. A viable health sector that can lead to better overall health is thus very important to a population and the HN government in supporting the stabilization and reconstruction efforts.

b. The term "health" is considered in the broadest sense as defined by the World Health Organization (WHO), "a state of complete physical, mental and social well-being, and not merely the absence of disease or infirmity." Thus, health includes direct care, disease surveillance and prevention, sanitation, nutrition, potable water, hazardous waste and material management, and consideration of physical and psychological impact of conflict and hardship. All of these components of health are typically disrupted, and often destroyed, in nations in which military operations are conducted or other natural or man-made crises have occurred. Many times these services were already in disrepair and a new emergency or conflict makes them even worse.

c. Other sectors of a society that overlap with and impact the health sector include governance, administration, logistics, economics, and security. The amount of HN governmental control over health infrastructure, policy, and personnel, or lack thereof, will determine how the health assets will be employed and if they can be reconstructed. A country's processes and alternative processes for acquiring medical materiel will be affected by its other logistic needs and capabilities. Finally, if the environment is insecure, the risk to health sector workers may prevent them from delivering services to the population.

3. Medical Civil-Military Operations

a. MCMO are accomplished by health support personnel and typically affect the health sector of the involved nation and where other civil sectors integrate with the health sector. Cooperation and coordination with joint military assets, interagency partners, HN, FN, IPI, NGOs, IGOs, private sector, and other entities will facilitate better long-term effects and outcomes.

b. **MCMO can be employed across the Range of Military Operations.** MCMO include peacetime medical engagement cooperation activities, FHA, disaster response and disease outbreak response in a permissive environment, pre-conflict health-related CMO, and health-related activities during major campaigns and operations, and post-conflict stability operations. Although the primary mission of health support is to enable FHP, health support personnel may be tasked to conduct or support MCMO in activities that build HN or FN capacity in the public health sector. These operations often are conducted in areas where social services have been disrupted, resulting in poor sanitation, inadequate and unsafe food and water (as well as distribution problems), civil disturbances, and general civil unrest, diseases, uncontrolled distribution of hazardous wastes and hazardous materials, and environmental extremes. In this environment, there are several health support activities that may be appropriate for MCMO that include public health activities, to include preventive medicine initiatives, personal sanitation and hygiene training, safe food and water preparation and handling, infant and child care, preventive dental hygiene, immunizations of humans and animals, veterinary care and behavioral health surveillance and support. Additional efforts can include the development of logistic programs, continuing medical support education programs and medical intelligence and threat analysis, and assistance in upgrading and devising methods for supplying and sustaining existing HN medical infrastructure and facilities.

4. Planning for Medical Civil-Military Operations

a. Medical planners must consider FHP and direct care needs of US forces as well as the assets and resources needed to support CMO designed for the indigenous population. For example, the medical planners may have to adjust typical personnel and logistic packages to care for women and children affected even in operations not originally of a humanitarian nature.

b. Medical planning should account for the appropriate MCMO that will enhance each type of operation and at each operational phase. The medical planner in conjunction with other experts within the joint force surgeon's office must liaise with the CMO staff, the HN or FN ministry of health, the country team, USAID, and other USG and international agencies that address the health sector to define requirements and capabilities; establish roles and responsibilities; identify the people, process, and technology necessary to conduct effective CIM; and provide functional area analysis to the commander. An understanding of the capabilities, intentions, and efforts of these organizations will allow the joint force surgeon and the medical planners to include, or exclude, joint US military health assets as appropriate.

c. Needs assessment should be conducted in conjunction with the HN or FN ministry of health or governance leadership in the health sector, when possible. Civilian health partners such as the Centers for Disease Control and Prevention, WHO, USAID, and any NGOs/IGOs familiar with the operational area can help with this process. The goal is to identify the health sector priorities of the HN or FN and the most threatening issues to the local population. In doing so, the medical health service can then target resources and health assets to projects that will help build indigenous health system capacity and capabilities, save lives, meet the commander's CMO objectives, and be sustainable by the HN or FN upon transition.

d. CMO planners need to be aware of aeromedical evacuation requirements in regard to highly contagious diseases. Patients with suspected or confirmed highly contagious diseases that pose a threat to US national security, require special public health action, or have the potential to cause public panic and social disruption will be treated in place and not transported with the aeromedical evacuation system. In extreme cases, there may be a requirement to move one or two index cases for medical evaluation or critical medical care. Immediate contact should be made with the supporting patient medical requirements center for the affected AOR to coordinate decisions for transport. If patient movement is required, prior approval must be given by the involved GCC, CDRUSTRANSCOM, and SecDef in consultation with medical authorities.

e. Medical logistics play a significant role in the delivery of health care during stability operations. Prior to a deployment, the joint force surgeon determines if there are any special medical supplies or equipment requirements for the operation; with the focus of providing only those supplies and medications available to the HN on a regular basis. Due to the variety of operations there will be different priorities to meet MCMO needs. The medical planner must include plans on how logistics experts will obtain and coordinate transportation, and transport, receive, sort, store, and distribute Class VIII materiel. Further, medical logistic personnel can collaborate with IGOs, NGOs, and the HN or FN in assisting the military or civilian medical supply infrastructure and industry. See Figure A-C-1 for CMO medical planning considerations.

5. **Caring for Non-United States Patients**

Past lessons in stability operations indicate that although providing care and medical resources to non-US patients has not been specifically planned for except in pure humanitarian missions, it is done in almost every operation. Populations that must be cared for include DCs, enemy wounded, and detainees. While under US control, enemy wounded and detainees are to receive medical treatment equivalent to that provided to US Armed Forces personnel within the AOR. Consequently, during planning efforts, careful consideration should be given to what role of care could be sustainable by the host-nation health sector for the care of local populations affected by US military actions. Often times, health care experts treat people in need regardless of the person's affiliation or combatant status.

Medical Planning Considerations in
Medical Civil-Military Operations

- Enhance host nation legitimacy
- Account and prepare for local cultural and religious norms
- Share information and validation of ideas with civil affairs, foreign area officers, and local and international health experts
- Recognize local and international standards of care and avoid raising expectations above what is sustainable by the host nation
- Account for potential negative effects of medical civil-military operations on local health care system and the economy
- Legal issues

Figure A-C-1. Medical Planning Considerations in Medical Civil-Military Operations

6. Health Sector Capacity Building

a. Health sector capacity building includes interventions with intent to rebuild indigenous capability and ownership in the health sector. The goal is to equip, or re-equip, the HN or FN to take care of their own people instead of the US military providing care and services of a different kind, quality, scope, and logistic package than what will be present upon transition. Basically, capacity building should avoid providing parallel medical support that foster different expectations or standards than HN or FN can sustain in the future.

b. Health sector capacity building should focus on public health and preventive medicine, which are the basis of a strong health sector. The most common causes of morbidity and mortality are addressed mainly with sanitation, potable water availability, and nutritious food availability. Direct medical care and ancillary health services have a role as well and the US military medical forces can partner with other agencies to do so. Capacity building includes planning for the transition of health services totally to HN or FN control with other long-term NA health sector entities in support, such as USAID, the Red Cross, NGOs, or IGOs.

c. The focus of medical support initiatives during MCMO is to improve HN or FN capacity to provide public medical services to its population, thereby enhancing legitimacy of the HN or FN, enhancing FP, and accomplishing the JFC's objectives. Capacity building initiatives during MCMO should emphasize long-term developmental programs that are sustainable by the HN or FN.

7. Teams

Multiple teams and cells can be established to bring military and civilian minds together, both indigenous and multinational, to coordinate and cooperate on CMO. Health/medical personnel can be members on these teams and function in advisory and planning capacities to help achieve success in the health sector that supports USG objectives. The health care experts on these teams may come from different USG departments and agencies including

DOD, USAID, the US embassy in the HN, Department of Health and Human Services, Public Health Service, Centers for Disease Control and Prevention, or NGO/IGO experts in MCMO and public health. Additionally, WHO and other regional or international health organizations may provide invaluable collaboration.

8. Joint Medical Assets for Civil-Military Operations

The five overarching joint medical capabilities for health support are: first responder care, forward resuscitative care, theater hospitalization, definitive care, and en route care. These capabilities are considered throughout the continuum of the health care system by the command surgeons and medical planners. MCMO is not one of these five listed capabilities, and there are no stand alone medical units from any Service primarily designated to accomplish MCMO. Theater medical assets must be designated to accomplish MCMO as an additional mission. However, capabilities are present within each Service that can adapt to providing civic assistance. There are a limited number of medical personnel within each Service who have acquired training and experience in CMO related activities and are well suited for leading, planning, and executing MCMO.

a. **USA.** CA units have medical personnel assigned with the duties of providing evaluation and advice on health sector issues pertinent to the CAO. Particular emphasis of the medical CA team member is placed upon preventive medicine sanitation and disease prevention, veterinary medicine and prevention of zoonotic diseases. CA health personnel are not intended to provide joint FHP, casualty care, or patient movement capabilities to the CA unit, nor deliver medical supplies to the populations to achieve CA objectives. Consequently, CA units are dependent on theater health support assets for the care of the CA unit and dependent upon theater health support assets in conjunction with HN and NGO assets to execute MCMO. USA battalion and brigade size units and higher contain attached or assigned Professional Filler System doctors, assigned physician's assistants and organic medical platoons and companies that can provide medical expertise to maneuver units conducting CMO.

b. **USN.** The Navy does not have any medical personnel or units primarily dedicated to MCMO or CA support. Hospital corpsmen in special operations have some CA training as do all SOF. Forward deployable preventive medicine units are ideally suited to assume a civic assistance role and accomplish collaborative MCMO with HN or FN and international assets. Navy hospital ships are capable of providing medical assets to a region for a defined period and in a visible fashion. These and other organic medical assets can be employed to provide civic assistance in various operations, but again should be employed with the planning principles noted previously into primarily capacity building activities with long-term sustainability and effects for the allies being supported.

For more information on hospital ships, see NTTP 4-04.6, Hospital Ships.

c. **USMC.** The AC Marine Corps CA force does not normally have a medical expert assigned on its table of organization, though the MAGTF normally deploys with its own organic medical capability which can be used in CMO.

d. **USAF.** The Air Force Medical Service (AFMS) deploys modular, expandable field health service units and equipment packages to accomplish care in expeditionary force operations. The AFMS provides an infrastructure designed to field and sustain a medically ready force throughout the entire range of military operations. This postures the AFMS to cover the full range of global engagement to respond in HA, disaster response, as well as health care operations. Due to the modularity and rapid deployment capability, AFMS assets may be used to support a primarily humanitarian, civic, or other multinational stability operations. AFMS personnel participate at the start of force employment planning and expeditionary force operations. Health service surveillance teams are critical assets in this process and can report on health threats at deployment locations. The USAF IHS program serves combatant and component command surgeons by providing medics with proficiency in a second language, regional and cultural expertise, medical planning, medical diplomacy, CMO, knowledge of IGOs and NGOs, knowledge of HA and disaster response, and other medical stability operations. IHS personnel assigned to CCMDs or to a JTF surgeon's staff work at the strategic and operational levels with CA to monitor and guide MCMO. IHS personnel from the AC and RC can lead or augment other health assets in tactical execution of MCMO.

ANNEX D TO APPENDIX A
MILITARY POLICE OR SECURITY FORCES

1. United States Army Military Police

a. MP demonstrate their competencies (soldiering, policing, corrections, and investigations) through the performance of its unique technical capabilities and tactical tasks. These technical capabilities and tactical tasks combine to form the MP disciplines (police operations, detention operations, and security and mobility support) (see Figure A-D-1), which enable the elements of combat power support the generating force and the operational Army across the range of military operations.

Army Military Police Disciplines and Technical Capabilities and Tactical Tasks		
Police Operations	**Detention**	**Security and Mobility Support**
Perform law enforcement	Confine United States military prisoners	Conduct movement support to mobility operations
Conduct traffic management and enforcement	Conduct detainee operations	Develop traffic regulation and enforcement plan
Conduct criminal investigation	Conduct host nation corrections training and support	Conduct enforcement of main supply route regulations
Provide customs support		Conduct a route reconnaissance
Restore and maintain order		Control movement of dislocated civilians
Support border control, boundary security, and freedom of movement		Conduct resettlement operations
Enable an interim criminal justice system		Conduct populace and resource control
Conduct host nation police training and support		Conduct reconnaissance
Provide support to civil law enforcement		Conduct surveillance
Conduct police engagement		Conduct operational area security
Employ forensic analysis or biometric identification capabilities		Conduct base/base camp defense
Evidence response team		Conduct critical asset security
Provide straggler movement control		Provide protective services for selected individuals
		Conduct response force operations
		Secure lines of communication, supply routes, and convoys
		Port and pier security
		Support area damage control
		Apply antiterrorism measures
		Implement physical security procedures
		Logistical security
		Crime prevention
		Military working dog

Figure A-D-1. Army Military Police Disciplines and Technical Capabilities and Tactical Tasks

b. The USA provides the JFC a complete range of MP organizations from theater-level MP commands, headed by a major general, through MP brigades task organized with two to five MP or MP detention battalions, to a variety of companies and teams. The MP battalion is the most versatile of the battalion headquarters, conducting all three MP disciplines, and is the only MP battalion-level element optimized to conduct those MP tasks that comprise the security and mobility support discipline. The MP detention battalion is designed with a focus on the MP tasks that comprise the detention operations discipline. When fully operational, the MP detention battalion may operate a detainee facility capable of detaining 4,000 detainees. Specialized MP teams include military working dogs and MP LE detachments. Each Army MP brigade is equipped with a nonlethal capability set to support each of its assigned missions providing an escalation of force capability.

c. The JFC is able to draw from a force pool of MP units available for integration into joint forces at various echelons. The theater army normally receives one MP command when more than one MP brigade is required. The MP force supporting a corps is not set by rules of allocation. Rather, the force is tailored to meet anticipated requirements based on an analysis of the situation. The MP brigade headquarters focuses on support to corps and echelon-above-corps operations. The MP brigade is capable of providing effective mission command of MP operations for contingencies in which a corps headquarters is required and is the most likely MP headquarters to be tailored for a corps echelon. The tailored MP force supporting a division is not set by rules of allocation. Rather, the force is tailored to meet anticipated requirements based on an analysis of the situation. The divisional MP force may be organized under a multifunctional headquarters, such as the maneuver enhancement brigade, or under a functional MP headquarters.

d. **United States Army Criminal Investigation Command (USACIDC).** USACIDC operations support the senior mission commander or GCC in maintaining discipline and order by preventing or investigating felony crimes which reduce a unit's ability to train and fight. During investigations, USACIDC concentrates efforts on serious crimes, such as wrongful deaths, controlled substance offenses, theft (based on the amount limit identified in Army Regulation 195-2, *Criminal Investigation Activities*), fraud, sexual misconduct, assaults, cyberspace crimes, and other national security offenses. USACIDC also conducts sensitive and special investigations involving senior Army officials and those associated with classified programs. USACIDC provides technical investigative support, integrating its organic capabilities with those of other federal investigative agencies, joint and combined police activities, Army MP activities, and other sources of MP-related reachback support.

For more information on US Army MP, see FM 3-39, Military Police Operations.

2. **United States Marine Corps**

a. Each MEF has a LE battalion assigned under the MEF headquarters group. The LE battalion provides task organized, functionally specialized police units, capable of conducting law and order functions to include LE, policing, police advising/training, and limited detentions/corrections operations tailored to support the operational requirements of the MAGTF commander. This provides optimal support to the entire MAGTF. There is a LE integration officer/chief assigned to the MEF command element and each major subordinate command to assist the commanders in coordinating and planning for LE support requirements.

b. The LE battalion provides the MAGTF commander the following capabilities:

(1) **LE Operations.** Those activities performed by personnel authorized by legal authority to compel compliance with, and investigate violations of, laws, directives, and punitive regulations. Key actions include:

(a) Provost marshals' office/police station operations.

(b) Traffic enforcement.

(c) Incident response.

(d) Investigations.

(e) Site exploitation.

(f) Identity operations support.

(g) Exploitation analysis operations.

(h) Customs/border control support.

(2) **Policing Operations.** The goal is the establishment, maintenance, or restoration of law, order, and safety through the employment of police techniques, methodology, principles, and capabilities during military operations. Key actions include:

(a) Police patrols.

(b) Police intelligence.

(c) Route regulation.

(d) Military working dog operations.

(e) Civil disturbance control.

(f) Protective services operations.

(3) **Police Advising/Training.** Advising and mission oriented training provided by MP personnel to enhance: Marine Corps units, external agencies, and HNs police/security forces to build their law and order capabilities. Specialized MP capabilities also serve to provide unique expertise as enablers to operations. Key actions include capabilities that encompass MP expertise that can advise and develop external units to assist in their mission accomplishment.

(4) **Limited Detainee/Corrections Operations.** Plan, coordinate, conduct, and monitor the collection, processing, safeguarding, and transfer of enemy prisoners of war, civilian internees, and US military prisoners. Included are actions taken to ensure that adequate shelter, sustainment, protection, and custody and control for detainee/corrections operations. Advise supported Service, interagency, multinational, and HN commands/agencies on detainee/corrections operations.

3. **United States Air Force**

   a. USAF security forces provide LE, security, and base defense in the following areas in support of USAF, joint, and multinational operations:

   (1) **Law and Order Operations.** Entry control and traffic control points, LE, crime prevention, traffic control, resource protection, and limited accident/incident investigation.

   (2) **Base Security Operations.** Countering enemy ground attacks on air bases is a common task for all security forces.

   (3) **Military Working Dogs.** The USAF trains DOD military working dogs at Lackland Air force Base, TX in support of its requirements as well as other DOD or USG taskings.

   (4) **Combat Arms.** Conduct small arms training and weapons maintenance.

   (5) **Nuclear Security.** Provide security for nuclear munitions from stockpile to deployment.

   (6) **Area Security Operations.** Security forces can conduct operations beyond the air base to provide protection against enemy attacks.

   c. Security forces conduct these missions throughout the USAF, CONUS, and outside the continental United States (OCONUS). Security forces conduct these missions fully armed and prepared to confront any threat against US national security.

   d. In OCONUS operations, the air base defense mission may include a base boundary that extends beyond the base perimeter in order to conduct tactical maneuver to defend against the threat of attacks using standoff weapons. Security forces conduct combat patrols outside the perimeter fence within the base boundary. Security forces coordinate these operations with local LE, or in a theater of war, with HN, FN, or MP assets. Security forces ensure the area of security for the base is understood and procedures to respond and reinforce the security forces are coordinated.

   e. The Air Force Office of Special Investigations (AFOSI) is a field operating agency that is the Air Force's felony-level investigative service. It reports to the Inspector General, Office of the Secretary of the Air Force. The AFOSI provides professional investigative service to commanders of all Air Force activities. It further identifies, investigates, and neutralizes criminal, terrorist, and espionage threats to the USAF and DOD personnel and resources. AFOSI focuses on four priorities: detect and provide early warning or worldwide threats to the USAF; identify and resolve crime impacting USAF readiness or good order and discipline; combat threats to USAF information systems and technologies; and detect and defeat fraud impacting USAF acquisitions and base level capabilities.

4. United States Navy

The Navy's maritime expeditionary security force (MESF) operations are aimed at countering or defeating Levels I and II threats and conducting MESF activities and operations that augment other forces in countering or defeating a Level III threat (threat levels are defined in JP 3-10, *Joint Security Operations in Theater*). The threat spectrum requires the conduct of maritime expeditionary security operations against diverse formations and capabilities to include terrorists engaged in espionage, sabotage, and subversion; small-scale, irregular forces engaged in unconventional warfare requiring the application of COIN techniques; and larger scale CF engaged in combat in multiple environments. The foundations of maritime expeditionary security rest in scalable, sustainable security forces capable of defending mission critical assets in any operating environment. USN MESF units and USCG deployable specialized forces conduct maritime and inshore surveillance, security, antiterrorism (AT), ground and afloat defense, and counterintelligence support of harbor defense (HD) and port security (PS) operations. In addition, these units are capable of accomplishing a wide range of secondary tasks from detention operations to LE. Maritime expeditionary security operations:

(1) Conduct security for designated assets.

(2) Provide layered defense in the integrated coastal and landward portion of the maritime domain.

(3) Provide maritime expeditionary C2 integration with the NCC; JFMCC; commander JTF; and multinational operations when directed.

(4) Provide the NCC/JFMCC with adaptive force packages responsive to the CCDR's force requirements.

(5) Support integrated maritime expeditionary security capabilities including:

(a) Mobile and fixed defensive positions.

(b) Visit, board, search, and seizure Levels I, II, and III.

(c) Security in support of NCC/JFMCC operations.

(d) HD/PS and harbor approach defense.

(6) Provide maritime interception operations intelligence exploitation teams.

(7) Provide maritime intelligence exploitation/sensitive site exploitation teams.

(8) Support NCC theater security cooperation activities providing:

    (a) Training capability for partnering with other nations.

    (b) Support for HN stability, security, transition, and reconstruction.

ANNEX E TO APPENDIX A
MILITARY INFORMATION SUPPORT OPERATIONS

1. United States Army

a. MISO are planned operations conveying selected information and indicators to foreign audiences and are intended to influence the emotions, motives, objective reasoning, attitudes, and ultimately the behavior of foreign governments, organizations, groups, and individuals. The purpose of MISO is to induce or reinforce foreign attitudes and behaviors favorable to US national policy objectives.

(1) MISO are vital to CMO in pursuit of US national and military objectives in support of the JFC across the range of military operations. Coordination, synchronization, and deconfliction of the other IRCs enhance MISO effectiveness. Dissemination of information about CMO efforts and results via MISO can affect the attitudes of broader audiences and favorably influence key groups or individuals. Conversely, CMO information about individuals and groups in the OE, conditions affecting their behavior, and other factors contribute to MISO development of effective messages and actions to influence selected target audiences.

(2) CDRUSSOCOM exercises COCOM of all active USA MIS forces; USA Reserve MIS forces are assigned to FORSCOM and further assigned to the USAR Command. When directed, CDRUSSOCOM and Commander, FORSCOM provide MIS units and personnel to CCDRs and US ambassadors. Coordination of MIS forces operations is typically conducted through a JMISTF operating directly under the JFC. The USA MIS capability consists of the Military Information Support Operations Command (a provisional component subordinate command of USASOC), and two active and two USAR MIS groups.

b. **Military Information Support Group (MISG).** The MISG plans, coordinates, and executes MISO at the strategic, operational, and tactical levels. A MISG is structured to support conventional and SOF deployed worldwide. It can operate up to two MIS task forces at the CCMD and the JTF level. A MISG typically contains the following organizations:

(1) **MIS Battalion.** MIS battalions provide cultural and linguistic expertise and are capable of providing simultaneous MISO to two or more organizations within the CCMD;

(2) **Special Operations Media Operations Battalion.** The special operations media operations battalion provides audio, visual, and audiovisual production, signal support, and broadcast capabilities to the MISG, MISTF, and tactical MIS units. The battalion can simultaneously support two separate operational areas at the CCMD level. Additionally, the Strategic Dissemination Company in the USAR provides tactical-level media support to conventional MIS forces;

(3) **Tactical MIS Battalion.** Tactical MIS battalions provide MISO to corps-level units and below and select special operations and conventional task forces at Army-level equivalent-sized units. The battalion develops, produces, and disseminates messages within

the MISO program guidance (themes, objectives, and target audiences) and as authorized by the series approval authority (CCDR or subordinate JFC). The primary capability of the battalion is the development and dissemination of MISO messages, and coordination for the execution of MIS actions. All USAR MIS battalions are configured as tactical MIS battalions.

c. In addition to supporting CMO, MISO support the other special operations missions: FID, unconventional warfare, direct action, and counterterrorism. MISO also contribute to special operations collateral activities and operations, such as humanitarian demining.

2. United States Marine Corps

The USMC maintains an organic capability to conduct tactical and limited MISO. The MIS capability resides principally with the Marine Corps Information Operations Center and is organized as a tactical MISO company with three deployable expeditionary military information support detachments (EMDs). Each EMD contains three expeditionary military information support teams (EMTs). USMC EMTs are routinely deployed in support of Marine Corps components; MAGTFs, particularly Marine expeditionary units embarked aboard amphibious shipping; and various US Army MIS organizations such as MIS teams or JMISTFs. EMTs can plan and execute MISO through face-to-face communication, loudspeaker operations, radio broadcasts using radio-in-a-box, and disseminating various print and novelty products to selected target audiences in support of a commander's objectives. Additionally, MV-22 Ospreys, KC-130 Hercules, and various helicopter assault support assets organic to a deployed MAGTF can conduct leaflet dissemination. The Marine Corps Information Operations Center can execute both audible and visible actions designed to convey specific impressions to the enemy (e.g., broadcasts from man-portable, vehicle-mounted, and airborne loudspeaker systems as well as radio-in-a-box frequency modulation and amplitude modulation band systems). Additionally, MV-22, KC-130, and helicopter assault support assets (organic to the Marine aircraft wings) can conduct leaflet dissemination.

3. United States Navy

a. Capabilities to produce audiovisual products are available from Navy Expeditionary Combat Camera; Fleet Combat Camera Group, Pacific; and from all aircraft carriers and most large deck amphibious warfare ships. Several sea-based Navy and USMC jet aircraft are configured to drop PDU-5/B leaflet canisters to dispense leaflets. Ships also have voice broadcast capabilities including high frequency, very high frequency, and ultra high frequency.

b. While product development is carried out almost exclusively by Army MISO planners, Navy personnel have the capability to produce documents, posters, articles, and other material for MISO. Language capabilities exist in naval intelligence and among naval personnel for most Asian, Middle Eastern, and European languages.

4. United States Air Force

a. The USAF has a variety of assets used to execute missions in support of MISO objectives. EC-130 COMMANDO SOLO aircraft are equipped to broadcast MISO radio and television products. Transport aircraft perform static line leaflet airdrop missions. USAF aircraft can dispense leaflets by dropping leaflet canisters.

b. USAF MISO capabilities extend beyond the traditional dissemination roles of airborne broadcasts and leaflet drops. Behavioral influences analysis (BIA) provides an analytical framework to facilitate understanding and exploitation of the perceptual and behavioral context of the OE. BIA directly supports MISO target audience analysis providing a more robust assessment of target audiences.

c. MIS officers coordinate and liaise between the Air Force air operations center (or joint air operations center if designated) and the IO staff to utilize all-source analysis of an adversary's sociological, cultural, and demographic information to recommend effective MIS strategies. USAF MIS forces fill individual billets on joint manning documents and are capable of providing direct support and general support roles to units conducting MISO.

For additional information, refer to JP 3-13.2, Military Information Support Operations.

Intentionally Blank

APPENDIX B
PLANNING CONSIDERATIONS FOR CIVIL AFFAIRS OPERATIONS

1. General

The JFC's CMO staff provides staff support of USA, USMC, and USN CA forces deployed in theater. They ensure that CA capabilities are employed and that CAO are synchronized with conventional military operations. CMO staffs also ensure CA personnel participate in theater mission planning and that theater component commanders are thoroughly familiar with CA capabilities in addition to operational and support requirements. TSOCs provide C2 of SOF deployed in theater. They ensure that SOF capabilities are employed and that SOF are synchronized with conventional military operations. TSOCs also ensure SOF personnel participate in theater mission planning and that theater component commanders are thoroughly familiar with SOF capabilities in addition to operational and support requirements.

2. Planning Considerations

a. **CA Selection.** Selection of CA in support of a plan or order should be based on a clear concept of CA mission requirements. Once requirements are developed, the CMO staff element should determine appropriate augmentation requirements based on CA functional expertise.

b. **Understanding the Civil Dimension.** The challenge to CMO planners is to articulate their contribution to the JFC's mission. These skills generally are not aligned with analysis needs in the conventional military. In the course of mission analysis, the COGs concept is useful as an analytical tool while designing campaigns and operations to assist commanders and staffs in analyzing friendly and adversary sources of strength as well as weaknesses and vulnerabilities.

(1) Analysis of the civil environment is necessary for CMO planning to identify strengths, weaknesses, opportunities, and threats in civil infrastructure, economy, governance, and other IPI that can be leveraged to advance the joint mission and USG objectives.

(2) Commanders and CMO planners must look beyond the traditional military construct in considering the impact of the civil dimension on operations. While the civil dimension applies to adversary, friendly, and environmental COGs, in some operations, it can dominate the focus of analysis. In such situations, the interactions between humans and the environment can result in recursive or unanticipated consequences. Additionally, analysis of the civil dimension is a continuous process throughout an operation and looks at the following six interrelated civil ASCOPE considerations:

(a) **Areas.** Key civilian areas are localities or aspects of the terrain within a commander's OE, which are not normally thought of as militarily significant. The commander must analyze key civilian areas in terms of how these areas affect the military's mission as well as how military operations impact these areas. Examples of key civilian areas that a commander should analyze are areas defined by political boundaries (e.g., districts within a city and municipalities within a region); areas that have historical or cultural significance (e.g., ancestral lands, burial grounds, archeological sites and settlements, and hunting, gathering, or grazing areas of settled or nomadic people); locations of government centers; social, political, religious, or criminal enclaves; agricultural and mining regions; economic and industrial zones; ethnic fault lines; trade routes; and possible sites for the temporary settlement of DCs or other civil functions. Failure to consider key civilian areas can seriously affect the success of any military mission.

(b) **Structures.** Existing structures take on many significant roles. Bridges, communications towers, power plants, and dams, are often considered high-value targets. Others, such as churches, mosques, and national libraries, and archeological structures are cultural sites that are generally protected by international law or other agreements. Hospitals are given special protection under international law. Other facilities with practical applications, such as jails, warehouses, schools, television and radio stations, and print plants may be useful for military purposes. Analyzing structures involves determining the location, functions, capabilities, application, and consequences of supporting military operations. Using a structure for military purposes often competes with civilian requirements for the same structure and requires careful consideration. Additionally, if exigent military operations require decisions whether or not to destroy specific structures, consideration must balance the short- and long-term effects of such actions.

(c) **Capabilities.** Capabilities can be analyzed from different levels. The analyst views capabilities in priority from the perspective of those required to save, sustain, or enhance life. Capabilities can refer to the ability of local authorities be they HNs or FNs, aggressor nations, or some other bodies—to provide key functions or services to a populace (e.g., public administration, public safety, emergency services, food, water, agriculture, and environmental security). Capabilities include those areas with which the populace needs assistance in revitalizing after combat operations (e.g., public works and utilities, public health, economics, and commerce). Capabilities also refer to resources and services that can be contracted to support the military mission (e.g., interpreters, laundry services, and construction materials and equipment). The HN or other nations may provide these resources and services.

(d) **Organizations.** These organizations are nonmilitary groups or institutions that influence and interact within the operational area. They generally have a hierarchical structure, defined goals, established operations, fixed facilities or meeting places, and a means of financial or logistic support. Some organizations may be indigenous to the area, such as church groups, fraternal organizations, patriotic or service organizations, labor unions, criminal organizations, and community watch groups. Other organizations may be introduced to the area from external sources, such as multinational corporations, interagency partners, IGOs, and NGOs.

<u>1</u>. The commander must be familiar with the organizations operating within the operational area (e.g., their activities, capabilities, and limitations). Additionally, the commander must understand how the operations of different organizations impact on the

command's mission, how military operations impact on organizational activities, and how organizations and military forces can work together towards common goals, as necessary.

2. The commander uses the CMOC to keep advised of all these issues.

(e) **People.** This general term is used to describe the nonmilitary personnel encountered by military forces during operations. The term includes all the civilians within an operational area as well as those outside this area whose actions, opinions, or political influence can affect the military mission. Individually or collectively, people impact military operations in positive, negative, or neutral manners.

1. There may be many different groups of people living and working within a given operational area. Like the discussion of organizations above, people may be indigenous to the area or introduced from external sources. An analysis of demographics should identify various capabilities, needs, and intentions of a specific population.

2. It is useful to study the historical, cultural, ethnic, political, economic, and humanitarian factors of a target population in order to understand the civil environment. It is critical to identify key communicators as well as the formal and informal communication processes used to influence a given population.

(f) **Events.** Events include routine, cyclical, planned, or spontaneous activities that significantly impact both civilian lives and military operations. Some civil events that affect organizations, people, and military operations are national and religious holidays, agricultural crop/livestock and market cycles, elections, civil disturbances, and celebrations. Other events are disasters from natural, man-made, or technological sources that create civil hardship and require emergency response. Examples of events precipitated by military forces include combat operations, deployments, redeployments, and paydays. Once the analyst determines which events are occurring, it is important to template the events and to analyze them for political, economic, psychological, environmental, and legal implications.

c. **Predeployment Planning**

(1) The early deployment of CA in the operational area can be a great force multiplier, setting the stage for the introduction of follow-on forces into an environment that has benefited from specialized interaction with the local population.

(2) The functional composition of CA varies with mission, availability, qualifications of CA, plus the supported commander's preferences.

(3) Mobilization of RC CA must be a consideration during predeployment planning.

(a) The USA, USN, and USMC all have authorizations for CA specialists. The majority of these CA authorizations are in the RC.

(b) USAR CA units normally arrive in theater 130 days after Presidential Reserve Call-up for contingencies or upon mobilization.

(4) Ensure agreement/arrangement is in place with the HN through the appropriate en route and operational area US embassies for personnel and aircraft diplomatic clearances to support CA arrival.

d. **Post-Conflict Operations.** Post-conflict activities typically begin with significant military involvement, and then move increasingly toward civilian dominance as the threat wanes and civil infrastructures are reestablished. US forces frequently will be in transition from one mission to another. The transitions may cause the US military to be engaged in several types of joint operations across the range of operations. Transitions at the conclusion of any major military operation require significant preparation, planning, and coordination between the interagency community, NGOs, IGOs, and the HN/FN government. US military forces, at the conclusion of hostilities, will support long-term US interests and strategic objectives including the establishment of security and stability in the region.

(1) Transition or termination occurs either upon accomplishment of the mission or as the President or SecDef so directs. CMO planners play a major role in transition and termination not only in the planning process (by establishing a transition mechanism) but also with assisting civilian organizations in clarifying their respective roles and responsibilities after US military forces leave the area. In order for reserve CA personnel to be used in this critical phase, their need must be identified early to allow for mobilization and deployment.

(2) Predetermined progress achievements along LOOs such as, availability of resources, or a specific date is the basis for transition or termination criteria. A successful harvest or restoration of critical facilities in the crisis area are examples of events that might trigger termination of the mission. An acceptable drop in mortality rates, a certain percentage of DCs returned to their homes, or a given decrease in threat activity is statistical criteria that may prompt the end of US military forces' involvement. Fulfilling transition criteria is accomplished by evaluating performance outcomes through MOEs to track progress along LOEs. Progress along LOEs under a LOO can be uneven, or the initial conditions can vary significantly, so the weight of each LOE in defining transition criteria for the LOO they fall under should reflect operational conditions and requirements.

(3) When other organizations (such as UN, NGOs, HN, FN, and IGOs) have marshaled the necessary capabilities to assume the mission, US forces may execute a transition plan.

(4) Transition may occur between the US joint force, another military force (e.g., United States, multinational, and affected country), regional organization, the UN, or civilian organizations. A detailed plan addressing the various functions and to whom they will transition will greatly reduce the turmoil typically associated with transition. A comprehensive transition plan includes specific requirements for all elements involved in the transition, summarizes capabilities and assets, and assigns specific responsibilities. A major aspect during transition is the movement of large numbers of military forces and civilians out of or within the operational area.

(a) An unclassified transition plan written in easily understood terms particularly is required when transitioning to nonmilitary organizations. Organizing the plan by specific functions (such as provision of food, restoration of facilities, and medical care) also enhances the transition.

(b) The joint force staff should periodically review the transition plan with all organizations that have a part in it. This will help ensure that planning assumptions are still valid, and determine if changes in the situation require changes in the transition plan.

(5) Termination plans should cover transition to post-disaster or emergency activities and conditions, as well as disposition of military forces. Orders and termination plans should be prepared simultaneously and in conjunction with the deployment plan, with the termination plan serving as a supporting plan to an order.

(6) **Transition Planning.** CMO planners play a major role in transition planning and may be the best group to perform this function because of their expertise. In order for these planners to accomplish this task, a clearly identifiable end state and transition or termination criteria for the operation must be developed. Transition groups are formed early in the planning process of the operation with regular meetings to update the transition plan input as to the current operational environmental. Transition planning begins with the end state in mind and results in a sustainable, durable structure/system. Transition to another organization occurs because a specific deadline, milestone, or end state has been met.

(a) Transition planning is an integral part of operation planning and mission analysis.

(b) Transferring control of an operation from US military to a nonmilitary organization or another military force requires detailed planning and execution. Mission analysis (analysis of mission statement), an identifiable end state, USG strategic plan for reconstruction, stabilization, or conflict transformation, and the national policy will all play an important role in the transition process. Transferring control of an operation is situation dependent and each one will possess different characteristics and requirements.

(c) Transition planning must be initiated during the initial phases of operation planning to ensure adequate attention is placed in this critical area—plan for transition when planning for intervention.

(d) As the redeployment phase for US military forces approaches, it is important to continue emphasizing FP. The redeployment phase can be the most hazardous because the tactical focus shifts toward redeployment and away from FP. (Note: Although all facets of the transition planning process are important, it is critical that personnel protection is a priority in planning through implementation of the plan. Protection of the force is easy to overlook, but doing so could have serious consequences.)

(e) Areas that will significantly impact the development of a transition plan are:

1. Identification of issues.

2. Key events (past and present).

3. Work required to accomplish the transition.

4. A thorough knowledge of the organization or force taking over control of the operation.

(f) The CMOC is heavily involved in the transition process. The CMOC prepares to hand over its role as the facilitator between US forces and IGOs, NGOs, other interagency organizations, and local government agencies. CMOC personnel prepare a transition plan that includes all ongoing projects and coordination, points of contact for all agencies with which the CMOC has worked, possible resources, and any other information that may facilitate the transition process. There is no standard format for a transition plan. However, several significant areas must be addressed. The best way to cover all the areas is by using the five-paragraph operation order format (situation, mission, execution, sustainment, and command and signal). The CMOC can support joint, combined, or single-Service operations from the strategic to the tactical level. In general, the CMOC is a structured coordination center in which transition planning is an essential activity.

(g) All CMO assets, identified by their interaction with the civil environment and involved in a mission, must be prepared to assist in the planning and execution of transition operations. The civil dimension may be the most complex portion of this process. It is imperative that all teams or sections conduct effective CIM to aid in the transition process. The transition process must be considered from the initial planning of the mission. CA play a major role in this planning process because of their functional expertise, regional focus, and ability to operate and facilitate activities with a variety of organizations. Figure B-1 depicts a sample checklist for transition planning.

(h) The transitional plan must be synchronized with the strategic guidance. All entities involved in the transition must have the same themes and discussion points to be relayed to the IPI, IGOs, NGOs, HN government, and any other major players. It is critical to ensure the population is informed of the transition, and understand why. This will aid in the prevention of destabilization of the HN once the transition element begins to depart and turn operations over to HN governmental agencies.

e. **FP**

(1) FP includes preventive measures taken to mitigate hostile actions against DOD personnel (to include family members), resources, facilities, and critical information. These actions conserve the force's fighting potential so it can be applied at the decisive time and place and incorporate the coordinated and synchronized offensive and defensive measures to enable the effective employment of the joint force while degrading opportunities for the enemy. FP does not include actions to defeat the enemy or protect against accidents, weather, or disease. Elements of FP include but are not limited to the following:

Sample Checklist for Transition Planning

- Who will determine when the transition begins or is complete?
- Have stated operational objectives been accomplished?
- Who will fund the transition?
- What is the new mission?
- What US forces, equipment, and/or supplies will remain behind?
- What will be the command relationship for US forces that remain behind?
- What will be the communications requirements for US forces that remain behind?
- Who will support US forces that remain behind?
- Can intelligence be shared with the incoming force or organization?
- Will new rules of engagement be established?
- Will ongoing operations (e.g., engineer projects) be discontinued or interrupted?
- Will the United States be expected to provide communications capability to the incoming force or organization?
- Will the incoming force or organization use the same headquarters facility as the joint force?
- What is the policy for redeployment of the joint force?
- Will sufficient security be available to provide force protection? Who provides it?
- How will the turnover be accomplished?
- Who will handle public affairs for the transition?
- Have redeployment airlift and sealift arrangements been approved and passed to the United States Transportation Command?

Figure B-1. Sample Checklist for Transition Planning

(a) **Chemical, Biological, Radiological, and Nuclear (CBRN) Defense.** Operations in a CBRN environment will require the employment of strategic and operational capabilities and policies that minimize or negate CBRN threats or hazards within an OE. CBRN threats include the capability to employ and the intentional employment of, or intent to employ, weapons or improvised devices to produce CBRN hazards. The employment or threat of CBRN weapons including TIM poses serious challenges to US military operations worldwide. Together with USG interagency partners and partner nations, the military will continue to invest in capabilities to identify, protect against, respond to, and mitigate the effects of CBRN threats and hazards. The reduction of CBRN threats and hazards through building partnership capacity with partner nations and preventing the proliferation of WMD are essential in the global environment.

For additional guidance on CBRN, refer to JP 3-11, Operations in Chemical, Biological, Radiological, and Nuclear (CBRN) Environments.

(b) **AT.** AT programs support FP by establishing defensive measures that reduce the vulnerability of individuals and property to terrorist acts, to include rapid containment by local military and civilian force. They also consist of defensive measures to protect Service members, civilian employees, family members, facilities, information, and equipment.

For further guidance on AT, refer to JP 3-07.2, Antiterrorism.

(c) **Security.** Security of forces and means enhances FP by identifying and reducing friendly vulnerability to hostile acts, influence, or surprise. Security operations protect flanks and rear areas in the operational area. Physical security measures deter, detect, and defend critical installations, facilities, information, and systems against threats from intelligence assets, terrorists, criminals, and unconventional forces. Measures include fencing and perimeter stand-off space, lighting and sensors, vehicle barriers, blast protection, intrusion detection systems and electronic surveillance, and biometric access control devices and systems. Physical security measures, like any defense, should be overlapping and deployed in depth.

For further guidance on physical security measures, refer to JP 3-10, Joint Security Operations in Theater.

(d) **Operations Security (OPSEC).** Effective OPSEC prevents adversaries (or potential adversaries) from gaining critical information concerning friendly operations, and enable the successful execution of all IRCs. The most effective OPSEC measures manifest themselves at the lowest level. Varying patrol routes, staffing guard posts and towers at irregular intervals, and conducting vehicle and personnel searches and identification checks on a set but unpredictable pattern discourage terrorist activity.

For further guidance concerning OPSEC, refer to JP 3-13.3, Operations Security.

(e) **LE.** LE aids in FP through the prevention, detection, response, and investigation of crime. A cooperative police program involving military and civilian or HN or FN LE agencies directly contributes to overall FP.

(f) **Personal Security.** Personal security measures consist of common-sense rules of on- and off-duty conduct for every Service member. They also include use of individual protective equipment, use of hardened vehicles and facilities, employment of dedicated guard forces, and use of duress alarms.

(2) **Planning for FP**

(a) JFCs and their subordinate commanders must address FP during all phases of contingency action planning. All aspects of FP must be considered and threats minimized to ensure maximum operational success. JFCs and their subordinate commanders must implement FP measures appropriate to all anticipated threats, to include terrorists.

(b) Supported and supporting commanders must ensure that deploying forces receive thorough briefings concerning the threat and personnel protection requirements prior to and upon arrival in the operational area.

(c) In addition, JFCs and their subordinate commanders must evaluate the deployment of forces and each COA for the impact of terrorist organizations supporting the threat and those not directly supporting the threat but seeking to take advantage of the situation.

(d) CA forces must address their particular FP concerns with JFCs. For example, it may be inappropriate and counterproductive for CA in full combat attire to conduct liaison with local officials. These type concerns should be addressed early in the planning process. Additionally, CA must address with JFCs how the various elements of FP impact on how they perform their mission.

(e) CA, because of their ability to work with the populace and their overall expertise, can provide JFCs insight into FP concerns before they become major issues.

(f) Intelligence support to FP consists of monitoring, reporting, and analyzing the activities, intentions, and capabilities of adversarial groups to determine their possible COAs. Detecting the adversary's methods in today's OE requires a higher level of situational understanding, informed by current and precise intelligence. This type of threat drives the need for predictive intelligence based on analysis of focused information from intelligence, LE, and security activities.

For more detailed discussion of FP, refer to JP 3-0, Joint Operations.

f. Joint Urban Operations

(1) In any operational area, most of the civil authority and the greater part of the population are likely to reside in one or more urban areas. Because of the numbers and density of civilians, any urban operation will require a significant CMO (CAO) effort on the part of the joint force.

(2) CMO conducted as parts of urban operations strive to achieve the same objectives as in other types of operations. These are:

(a) Enhance military effectiveness.

(b) Support national objectives.

(c) Reduce the negative impact of military operations or other destructive force on civilians.

(3) CMO and Urban Operations

(a) As with other activities, the complex, physical aspects of urban terrain can hamper CMO. The urban terrain can fragment and channel CMO efforts, particularly FHA. It will be difficult to find and reach all those in need of support. Constricted terrain makes it more difficult to control large numbers of people in PRC operations. Urban areas normally offer many buildings usable for shelter, medical care, and other forms of support, but the damage to those structures from military operations or natural or man-made disaster can make them unusable, thus adding to the support difficulties.

(b) The civilian population is a primary concern of CMO, and urban areas may contain huge numbers of civilians. These numbers may range from the thousands to the millions. Depending on the circumstances, many will be displaced and in need of basic support. Services may be degraded or nonexistent. The requirement to control and support the noncombatant population can easily overwhelm local capabilities. Effective urban CMO requires knowledge of the ethnic, cultural, religious, and attitudinal characteristics of the populace. Noncombatant populations in urban areas are rarely homogenous, therefore effective CMO will require the understanding of neighborhoods, tribal relations, and the basic allegiances and daily life of the inhabitants.

(c) Urban infrastructure may be functioning with some degree of effectiveness, in which case CMO must work through and with local authorities and services. It may be necessary to repair physical infrastructure facilities and means, such as power plants or water stations, as part of CMO. Existing service infrastructure may be totally lacking or overwhelmed by circumstances, requiring the joint force to provide not only basic subsistence and shelter, but the full gamut of support personnel—police, legal, administration, engineer, sanitation, medical, transportation, and other.

(d) The proximity of civilians to military targets increases the requirement to actively screen the joint integrated prioritized target list for indirect fires and minimize the impact of collateral damage. The proximity to civilians increases the risks that diseases and other public health hazards will pose health risks to military personnel.

(4) **CMO Considerations in Joint Urban Operations.** Urban operations will include CMO. Urban CMO can support overall operational objectives or be the main focus of operations, but are in any case the responsibility of the CCDR to plan and conduct.

(5) **Planning Considerations.** Planning for CMO support of urban operations is generally the same as for other CMO with special emphasis on the nature of the urban area. The JFC and staff should consider the impact of military operations on noncombatants to include their culture, values, and infrastructure; thereby viewing the urban area as a dynamic and complex system—not solely as terrain. General planning considerations were addressed earlier in this chapter. Additional planning considerations are below:

(a) CMO planners should carefully consider these aspects of the urban area—terrain, civilian populace, environment, and infrastructure.

(b) Some other factors to consider include legal implications, communications, culture, education, economic, religious, labor, health, and administrative infrastructure.

(c) NGOs, IGOs, the interagency community, and IPI also play a major part in all CMO but may be of more importance in urban operations.

(6) **Synchronization.** CMO must be synchronized both internally and with other operations. The relation of CMO to the overall operation can vary a great deal depending on the situation. Joint urban operations could require the full extent of CMO in one portion of an urban area while another is still being heavily contested. Most likely, regardless of the situation, civilians in the operational area will have a great impact on operations. Planning must be synchronized to ensure CMO and other operations (e.g., combat operations) support the USG overall objectives.

(7) **Support.** CMO may require support in a number of key areas from other forces (e.g., health support, engineer, and MP/security forces).

(8) **Other Operational Considerations.** The most important urban operation consideration is that CMO will most likely occur simultaneously with, not subsequent to, other operations—including combat. The JFC must therefore identify sufficient forces and synchronize the planning and execution of these operations as well as the support required. The relation of CMO to other operations in joint urban operations will vary, but CMO will be a significant part of any operation.

For further guidance concerning urban operations, refer to JP 3-06, Joint Urban Operations.

g. **FCM**

(1) FCM is USG activities to assist friends and allies with preparing for and responding to a CBRN incident that occurs on foreign soil in order to mitigate human casualties and to provide temporary associated essential services. These operations involve those essential services and activities required to manage and mitigate problems resulting from disasters and catastrophes, including natural, man-made, or terrorist incidents. Such services may include transportation, communications, public works, fire fighting, information planning, care of mass casualties, resources support, essential or routine health and medical services, urban search and rescue, hazardous materials, food, and energy.

(2) Primary responsibility for managing and mitigating the effects of a FCM incident resides with the HN government. The DOS is designated as the primary agency for FCM operations in support of a foreign government. All DOD support will be coordinated through the responsible US embassy COM and country team.

For further detail concerning FCM, refer to Chairman of the Joint Chiefs of Staff Instruction (CJCSI) 3214.01B, Military Support to Foreign Consequence Management Operations, *JP 3-29,* Foreign Humanitarian Assistance, *JP 3-40,* Countering Weapons of Mass Destruction, *and JP 3-41,* Chemical, Biological, Radiological, and Nuclear Consequence Management.

h. **Humanitarian Demining Operations.** The general role of CA in these types of operations is to assist the assigned SOF and other forces in their efforts in supporting USG and geographic CCMDs in achieving their objectives.

(1) CA execute programs that build capabilities in management, administration, logistics, equipment maintenance, communications, and data processing. CA are instrumental in the establishment of the HN humanitarian demining office and the coordination of support with NGOs and IGOs.

(a) Special forces teams train HN cadre in techniques to locate, identify, and destroy landmines and unexploded ordnance.

(b) MIS teams assist HN governments to develop and implement mine awareness programs to train local populations to identify, avoid, and report locations of landmines and unexploded ordnance until these threats are removed.

(c) CA train the HN demining headquarters in management and C2 of its subordinate elements. CA also provide liaison with the USG, IGOs, NGOs, and local organizations to coordinate support of the HN or FN demining infrastructure.

(2) CA possess the expertise to support other SOF, CF, and civilian organizations in humanitarian demining operations. CA possess the unique skills that foster relationships with the civilian community, which allow them to be a logical choice as part of a team to assist HNs or FNs in demining operations.

For further guidance on military support to humanitarian demining operations, refer to CJCSI 3207.01B, Military Support to Humanitarian Mine Actions, *JP 3-15,* Barriers, Obstacles, and Mine Warfare for Joint Operations, *JP 3-29,* Foreign Humanitarian Assistance, *JP 3-40,* Countering Weapons of Mass Destruction, *and JP 3-41,* Chemical, Biological, Radiological, and Nuclear Consequence Management.

i. **Negotiation and Mediation.** Although negotiation normally is not a primary responsibility for CA, often it falls upon them. CA often find themselves in the role of a mediator or even arbitrator at some point during military operations. Each role requires different attributes, but there are many common ones and the following focuses on those common attributes and techniques. The COM is the lead USG representative in-country and must authorize JFC personnel to coordinate with HNs, IGOs, and NGOs.

(1) Negotiations do not occur in a vacuum. It is important to understand the broader issues of conflict and their changing nature.

(a) In many operations, it is essential to maintain dialogue with all parties, groups, and organizations—including of course the government if one exists, but also the opposition or various factions or militias.

(b) It is also important not to allow any one incident to destroy dialogue (even if force is applied)—creating an atmosphere of hostility will not lead to a resolution.

(2) Negotiation is an exercise in persuasion. It is a way to advance the command's interests by mutually decided action. Cooperation of the other parties is a must; consider them partners in solving problems.

(3) Think carefully about the full range of the force's interests and prepare thoroughly for the full range of interests of the other parties. What are the underlying interests behind a particular position that a party has taken on a particular issue? People negotiate for different reasons such as:

(a) Tasks (e.g., the lease of a compound);

(b) Relationships (e.g., to get to know the other party and find out more information about whom that person is); and

(c) Status (e.g., legitimacy as a participant in the eyes of others).

(4) Think carefully about alternatives in negotiating an agreement. How will you as a negotiator be most persuasive in educating others to see a negotiated settlement as being in their best interests?

(5) Be attuned to cultural differences. Actions can have different connotations. The use of language can be different; "yes" may mean "no". How people reason and what constitutes facts and what principles apply are shaped by culture. Solutions often are best when they come from the factions themselves. Nonverbal behavior such as the symbolic rituals or protocols of the arrangement for a meeting also is important. It is particularly important to look at opportunities for small interim agreements that can be seen as "trust building" steps that are necessary when it will take time to reach agreement on larger issues.

(6) Negotiations will be conducted at several levels: negotiations among USG departments and agencies; between the multinational partners; between the joint force and UN agencies; and between the joint force and local leaders. This complex web of negotiations requires the following to build consensus: tact, diplomacy, honesty, open mindedness, patience, fairness, effective communications, cross-cultural sensitivity, and careful planning.

(7) **Procedures for Negotiation.** Successful negotiations should be based on the following steps:

(a) Establish communications. The first step is to establish an effective means of communicating with the political or faction leader(s). Do not assume that certain leaders or elements are opposed to your efforts without careful investigation. Insist on fact finding before forming any opinions.

(b) Carefully develop a strategic plan and diagram the results of your analysis. Useful questions to answer in this analysis are:

1. What are the main issues?

2. Who are the relevant parties? First order? Second? Third?

3. What are these parties' publicly stated positions? Privately stated positions?

4. What are the underlying interests behind these positions?

5. What are the bottom-line needs of each party?

6. What are their concerns? Fears? To what degree does "historical baggage" affect them?

(c) There will be a negotiation on the conduct of negotiations (examples: physical location/seating arrangements [round table, U-shaped, etc.]/agenda/security requirements). This process must be addressed in the initial planning sessions.

(d) Set clear goals and objectives. Know what the joint force is trying to accomplish as well as the limits of its authority. Think carefully about how the joint force wants to approach the issues. Settle the easy issues first. Settle issue by issue in some order. Look to create linkages or to separate nonrelated issues. For example, security issues might be separated from logistic issues. Consider having details worked out at later sessions with the right people. Understand these sessions also will be negotiations.

(e) Work with the parties to identify common ground on which to build meaningful dialogue. Expect to spend considerable time determining the exact problem(s). At this stage, be problem-oriented rather than solution-oriented.

1. If a party perceives more benefits from an alternative to negotiations than to any outcome negotiations could produce, do not expect that party to negotiate to achieve an agreement. You need to educate and persuade them that negotiations will in fact produce the most benefits.

2. Focus on underlying interests. Differences in the relative value of interests, forecasts of future events, aversion to risk, and time preferences may offer opportunities to develop options for mutual gain.

3. Learn from the parties. Seek ways through partnering with them to find possible alternatives beyond their present thinking.

4. When necessary, assume the role of convener, facilitator, or mediator. Be patient.

(f) Composition of negotiating forum and decision-making mechanisms. In some cases a committee or council can be formed with appropriate representation from the various interested parties. It is critical to identify the right participants in advance. For example, will it include COM and JFC-level, mid-level, or working-level personnel?

1. In deciding what constitutes the appropriate construct for a meeting, consider the culture. For example, what role do women play in the society? How is status defined in the culture?

2. Composition of the committee or council also may include legal advisors, political representatives (e.g., DOS, UN agencies, or others), military representatives, and other civilian representatives from the joint force, NGOs, or IGOs.

3. Members should possess the status and ability to deal with the leadership representing all involved parties.

4. For those members seen as part of the joint force, it is important that they understand the issues and speak with one voice. This will require a prior coordination within the joint force's delegation. They must understand policy and direction from higher authority.

5. Negotiations are time-consuming and can be frustrating. As the head negotiator, be attentive to whether you have the people negotiating who can effectively recommend that their superiors ratify an agreement reached. Are all the decision makers who will determine whether the agreement reached is implemented represented in the committee or council?

6. A supportive climate needs to be developed for the decision makers to complete an agreement. In that vein, it is useful to talk to those who are not decision makers but from whom the decision makers will need support. In this way, they may assist you in helping their decision makers reach agreement.

7. In zones of severe conflict and state collapse, it is frequently difficult to determine the legitimate community leaders with whom any lasting agreement must be made.

8. The JFC must ensure that all of his or her negotiators understand the scope and latitude of their authority. Their requirement to obtain the JFC's prior approval will empower them in their role as negotiator or mediator.

(g) Establish the venue. What is the manner in which meetings can be called? Can a neutral ground be found that is acceptable to all sides? Should US representatives go to the factional leader's location, or will this improperly affect the negotiations? What about the details such as the seating arrangements or specific settings traditionally used in the culture?

1. Selection of a negotiating venue also should be based on security for all involved parties, accessibility, availability of communications facilities, and comfort.

2. Ensure that appropriate information arising from, or relevant to, the negotiations is shared with all parties. The timing of this sharing may vary depending on the circumstances.

3. Sharing of information notwithstanding, all information generated from the negotiations may be held in confidence until officially released. That decision will depend on the nature of the talks. For example, if publicity may help create support and empower the negotiators to agree, release of information may be constructive. Flexibility is needed here rather than a hard and fast rule.

(h) Cultural Considerations

1. There are organizational cultures within the various agencies and departments of the USG that shape the context of negotiations. Equally important are national cultural differences.

2. It is imperative that experienced interpreters be part of the negotiating team. What is critical is their understanding of the cultural context of terms used. The team needs more than literal translators.

3. Negotiation is only one means of resolving conflict. It is worthwhile to consider indigenous conflict resolution techniques in selecting an approach. Adapting your techniques to indigenous ones (degradation of US objectives is not acceptable) may improve the prospects for a settlement.

4. There are differences in styles of reasoning, manner in which an individual negotiates, who carries authority, and behavior in such dimensions as protocol and time. For example, in our culture it is accepted that one may offer concessions early in a negotiation to reach an agreement. That approach may not have the same connotation in other cultures. Moreover, the concept of compromise, which has a positive connotation for Americans, may have a negative one in other cultures.

5. Where we as Americans tend to be direct problem solvers with a give-and-take approach, other cultures are indirect, most concerned with the long-term relationship, historical context, and principles. Issues of symbolism, status, and face may be important considerations.

6. For example, answers may not be direct, forcing the negotiator to look for indirect formulations and nonverbal gestures to understand the other party's intent. In turn, careful wording and gestures are required so that unintended meanings are not sent. The other party may not say "no" directly to a proposal, but that is what is meant.

7. If agreement cannot be reached, it is still important to keep the dialogue going. The negotiator should at a minimum seek agreement on when the parties will meet again; anything to keep the momentum alive. It is often helpful to go back to earlier discussions on common ground and seek to keep trust alive in the process.

8. Within the negotiating team, one person who understands conflict dynamics and cross-cultural issues should look at the process of the negotiations and advise the rest of the team. This individual can watch for body language and other indicators of how the process is working. In turn, they may be able to coach the joint force negotiators in more effective techniques.

(i) Social Considerations

1. Social identity can be described through national, tribal, clan, religious, language, or other faction sharing the same geographical territory and subject to the same political authority and dominant cultural expectations, and that hold the same psychological ideals, beliefs, and convictions. Rapidly identifying the importance the leading social identity will directly reflect on the viability of rules established that are in conflict with general prescribed law by the current governing power (i.e., HN government).

2. Identification of the underlying causes of conflict among the civilian populace (social, economic, geographical, ethnic, religious, political) as related to the social economic aspects consider the populace and whether they feel secure. Corruption (example: involvement in illicit drug production/sale/transport, black marketing, banking system, social economic aspects). Consider the populace in reference to the level of security they feel is present.

<u>3.</u> It is worthwhile to consider essential needs (water, food, shelter, etc.) as a driving factor in stability operations. If necessities are unavailable, all good intentions will still lead to fear and resentment on the part of the locals.

<u>4.</u> Degree of religious freedom.

<u>5.</u> Presence of terrorist groups that could and do have an impact on the social fabric of the population (fear, compassion toward said group[s]).

<u>6.</u> Consider the overall quality of life (pros and cons).

(j) Implementation

<u>1.</u> At the conclusion of negotiations, a report should be prepared to ensure all accomplishments, agreements, and disagreements are recorded for future use.

<u>2.</u> Consider giving one person the task of reporting and presenting to all participants what has taken place. This can build trust in the process if it is viewed as an honest effort to understand each side's position.

Intentionally Blank

APPENDIX C
CIVIL INFORMATION MANAGEMENT

1. Description

a. Civil information pertains to civil ASCOPE within the civil component of the OE, which can be fused or processed to increase situational awareness and understanding and enhance unity of effort among interagency partners, coalition, HN, IGO, NGO, and IPI partners. It is a CA planning consideration.

b. CIM is the process whereby civil information is gathered, entered into a database, analyzed, and internally fused with other data sources from the supported element, higher headquarters, interagency, multinational, HN, IGO, NGO, and IPI partners. This process ensures the timely availability of accurate information for mission analysis. It also ensures the widest possible dissemination of civil information to other military and select nonmilitary partners throughout the JOA at the discretion of the JFC. CIM is not solely the task of the CA officer or noncommissioned officer in the CIM cell. It is an essential task for all components of a CA unit in coordination with the J-2, and should be broadly tasked to the supported units intelligence and maneuver elements to enhance the COP and facilitate the JIPOE process. The CIM goal is the enhancement of situational awareness and understanding for all elements in the OE to enhance decision making.

c. The primary purpose of CIM is to improve the commander's awareness and understanding of the civil component of the OE. The effective management of civil information provides a readily available historical database of geospatially referenced data that is collated and processed to support fusion and detailed analysis essential for mission planning. Civil information is gathered through civil assessment and survey, data mining, and collaboration. Examples of civil information consist of, but are not limited to CMO reports, situation reports, civil assessment and survey reports, village assessments, reports on key leader and other civil engagements, civil system assessments, reports on civil projects, and other logs, files, briefings, and photos pertaining to the civil environment (see Figure C-1).

d. Although CIM is a core task of CA, the joint force comprises many elements that interact with the civil population. During mission planning cycles, CAO and CMO planners must actively engage other members of the joint community to extend the reach and influence of civil information collection efforts. These elements include, but are not limited to, maneuver units and force enablers such as MP, engineers, chaplain, SJA, medical service, MISO, and civil-military teams.

e. Anticipating and satisfying civil information needs for the JFC are tasks for the CAO/CMO planners. The CMO planner is responsible for providing the key civil considerations that should support the JFC's intent in order to perform the following:

(1) Produce the CMO estimate.

(2) Participate in mission planning cycles.

```
Examples of Civil Information Reports and Assessments

  ● Civil-military           Types of Civil Data Assessment Forms
    operations reports        Building
  ● Situation reports         School/orphanage
                              Warehouse
  ● Capacity assessments      Store/market
  ● District/village          Arts/historical/cultural/religious
    assessments               Fuel point
                              Police station/security unit
  ● Project assessments       Fire station
                              Trash removal
                              Sewage
                              Hospital/clinic
                              Road/route reconnaissance
                              Bridge
                              Railway
                              Fishery/hatchery
                              Ports/harbors
                              Airfield
                              Farm
                              Veterinary
                              Water/well/dam
                              Dislocated civilian
                              Foreign humanitarian assistance/disaster relief
                              Key leader engagement
```

Figure C-1. Examples of Civil Information Reports and Assessments

(3) Write the CA annex (Annex G to operation plans/operation orders).

(4) Participate in CMO working group and IO working group to develop unity of effort across the JTF.

(5) Develop and synchronize the civil information plan with other efforts to satisfy the commander's information requirements.

(6) Develop the civil layers of the COP.

(7) Increase the JFC's situational awareness and understanding of the civil component of the operating environment.

(8) Coordinate and synchronize USG CMO efforts with the coalition, HN, NGOs, IGOs, and IPI.

(9) Develop standard operating procedures for the storage, maintenance, access, assurance, and sharing of civil information.

2. Organization and Employment

a. The responsible CMO staff manages the civil information process for the JFC and coordinates the retrieval, storage, dissemination, assurance, and access with appropriate staff information managers. Utilizing theater-specific CIM architectures, their supporting networks, and information assurance requirements as early as possible enables effective communication and coordination with other USG partners, IGO, NGO, and IPI operating in the JOA.

b. At each echelon, the CIM cell is the focal point for the consolidation of civil data and the development of geospatially referenced civil information. With available analytic capabilities, the O&I cell, organic to the CMOC, CIM cell focuses analysis on identifying civil vulnerabilities and their root causes. Once entered into the COP, the civil layers help shape operations and focus available resources to meet specific strategic and operational goals.

c. The CIM cell may be task organized in a CMOC or relocated within a JTF, JSOTF, or TSOC as dictated by the mission. Regardless of the episodic nature of the mission, the civil information will continue to have value throughout each phase of an operation or campaign.

d. The coordinated management of civil information is applicable across the range of military operations. Emphasized by the difficult experiences of both Iraq and Afghanistan, success is not only defined in military terms. CIM is critical in providing information and analysis in support of efforts for rebuilding infrastructure, supporting economic development, establishing the rule of law, building accountable governance, establishing essential services, and building a capable HN military responsible to civilian authority.

e. Commanders must ensure civil information and resultant products are accessible and available throughout the JFC and with other USG departments, agencies, and partner nations supporting disaster response and HA activities, development activities, and post-conflict reconstruction and stabilization activities.

f. Through collaboration, interagency, coalition, IGOs, NGOs, and IPIs operating within the JOA can provide additional sources of civil information. Collaboration contributes to successful military operations by unifying and synchronizing concurrent efforts to focus on a desired end state. Institutional and cultural differences may contribute to barriers in collaboration and information sharing between agencies; however, in most cases non-USG organizations and the USG are working toward similar goals. By attempting to accommodate these concerns and sharing useful information and resources, the JFC, can help encourage active IGO and NGO cooperation. This requires the JFC to manage and make available relevant information to appropriate stakeholders. To accomplish this, the CIM cell must identify existing architectures (not organic to the CIM cell) to host civil information at the appropriate classification level to support concurrent non-DOD efforts. To maximize information sharing to the greatest extent possible, the goal for civil information hosting should always begin at the lowest possible classification level while enabling civil information migration to provide echelon appropriate civil analysis (Figure C-2).

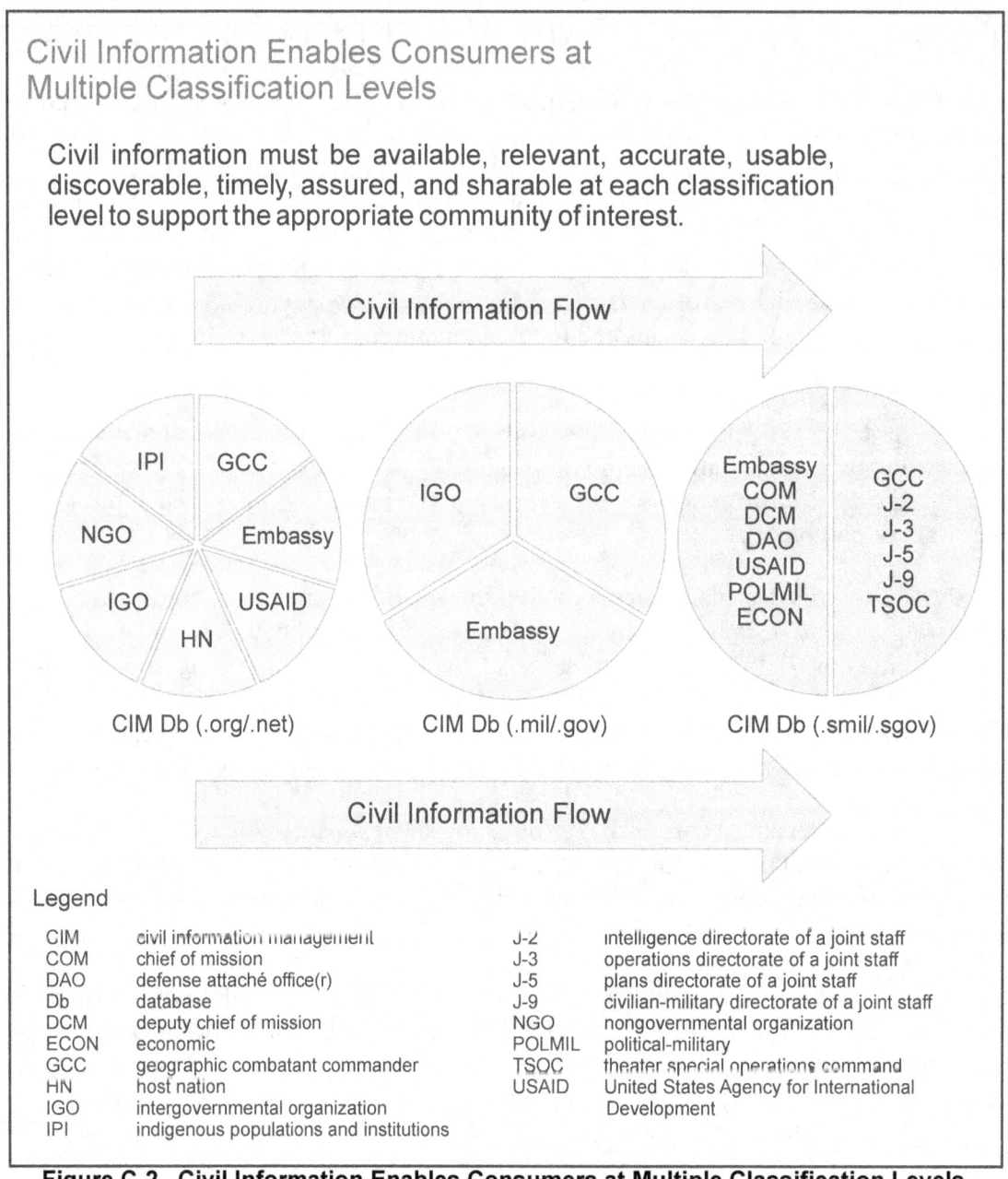

Figure C-2. Civil Information Enables Consumers at Multiple Classification Levels

g. The CIM process requires the ability to protect civil information by ensuring its integrity, authentication, confidentiality, and non-repudiation. However, electronic communication with HN and other partners may not be possible using the same rigor expected of DOD systems.

h. CIM sharing requires communication and understanding among the various centers, commissions, staffs, augmentations, field offices, and agencies. The management of civil information is a component of the joint IM plan and requires close coordination between the J-9 and the communications system directorate of a joint staff to address network architectures and interfaces, adherence to information assurance policies and compliance with DOD directives regarding the handling and distribution of information. The joint force must understand these policies and maintain communications with stakeholders to resolve issues as they arise.

3. CIM Process

The CIM process generates civil information through the following six steps (Figure C-3):

(1) Plan and Collaborate

(a) Mission planning should not be based solely on the staff's analysis of DOD-sourced information. Input from other sources, such as various intelligence organizations, interagency, the HN, IPI, IGOs, and NGOs is essential to developing a better understanding of the civil dimension. The CA staff leverages these external sources of information to provide a comprehensive understanding of the OE that enables the JFC to conduct operations that mitigate sources of instability, address civil vulnerabilities, and promote unity of effort.

(b) JFC participation in interagency and multinational forums with the command, senior USAID representatives, and other senior agency representatives are important for the deconfliction and coordination of activities.

(c) The JFC should participate in appropriate national-level formal and informal discussions among HN, UN, other government departments and agencies, and NGO participants to share perspectives and develop a common understanding.

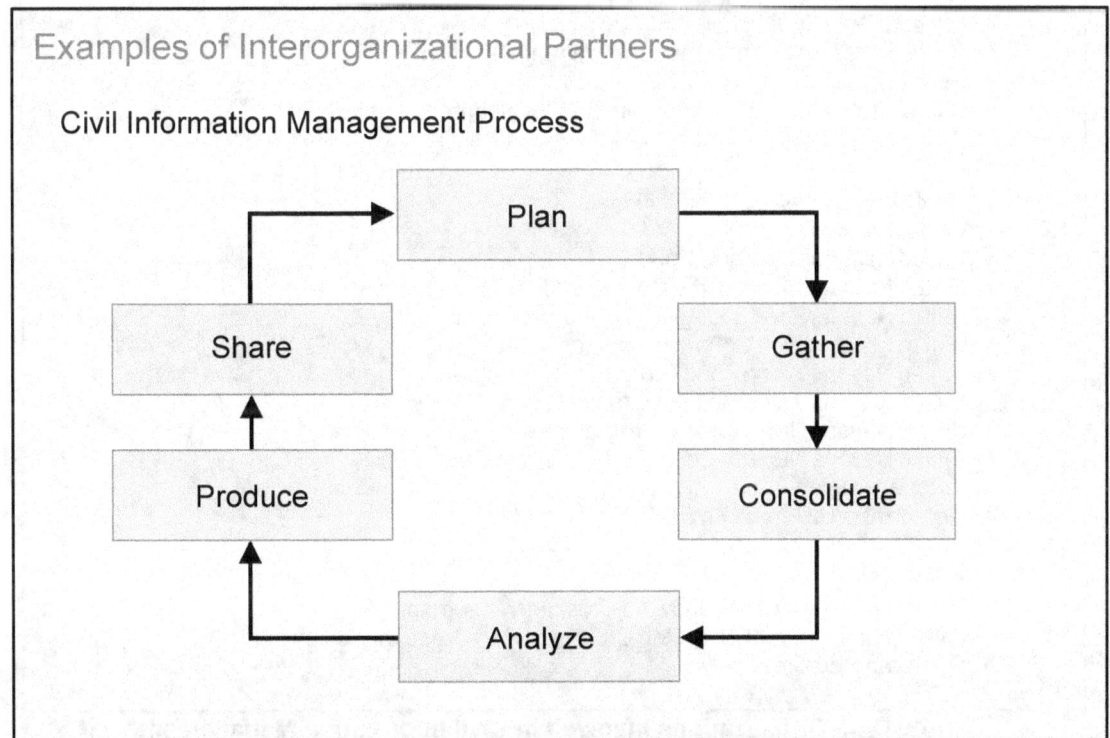

Figure C-3. Examples of Interorganizational Partners

(d) The establishment of, or participation in, CMOCs, an HA coordination center, a UN on-site operations coordination center, or other operational and tactical level collaboration and information sharing organizations by the joint force is essential for developing a comprehensive understanding of the OE among those conducting CMO (Figure C-4).

(e) Effective CIM requires the conduct of assessments to determine conditions in the JOA. Interagency, coalition, HN, NGO, IGO, and IPI support for these assessments may be critical to their accuracy. This assessment process serves two important purposes: to

---

Organizations Involved in Civil Information Management

United States Government (USG), Intergovernmental Organization (IGO), and Nongovernmental Organization (NGO) Interorganizational Coordination

USG Departments and Agencies
- Department of Agriculture
- Department of Commerce
- Department of Defense
- Department of Energy
- Department of Health and Human Services
- Department of Homeland Security
- Department of Justice
- Department of Labor
- Department of State
- Department of Transportation
- Department of the Treasury
- Central Intelligence Agency
- Environmental Protection Agency
- General Services Administration
- National Security Council
- Office of the Director of National Intelligence
- Peace Corps
- United States Agency for International Development

IGOs
- North Atlantic Treaty Organization
- United Nations
- United Nations Children's Fund
- United Nations Office for the Coordination of Humanitarian Affairs
- United Nations Food and Agriculture Organization
- United Nations High Commissioner for Refugees
- United Nations World Food Programme
- United Nations World Health Organization
- United Nations Development Programme
- United Nations Department of Peacekeeping Operations
- European Union
- Organization of American States

NGOs
- International Red Cross and Red Crescent Movement
- International Federation of Red Cross and Red Crescent Societies
- American Red Cross

Figure C-4. Organizations Involved in Civil Information Management

---

gain clarity of the current situation and to enable the HN government to be aware of the benefits of the transformation process proposed. There is a need for initial discussion between the international community and national actors about the scope and objectives of the assessments. These will be determined by a number of factors, including the openness, willingness, and capacity of the key HN leaders. Assessments provide an important opportunity to build trust between international and local people and organizations and to develop local ownership of assistance programs.

(2) **Information Gathering**

(a) Information gathering occurs at all levels through civil assessment and survey operations and data mining with interagency, coalition, HN, IGOs, NGOs, and IPIs to satisfy the JFC's requirements.

(b) The intent of CIM is to keep most of this information unclassified and easily shared with non-USG partners. The heart of information gathering is the daily interaction among US forces and the myriad of civilians in the supported commander's AO and the capture of these contacts and data points. Initial assessments may be short and superficial due to pressure to quickly design and implement programs and activities. Political priorities or immediate threats posed by natural disasters and ongoing or threatened violent conflict may obstruct in-depth planning and preparation at the onset of design and planning. If priorities or threats limit the ability to conduct a comprehensive assessment at the outset, initial plans should direct the completion of more detailed and comprehensive assessments as soon as possible.

(c) CR is a targeted, planned, and coordinated observations and evaluations of specific civil aspects of the environment. CR focuses on the civil component, the elements of which are area, structures, capabilities, organizations, people, and events. CR also focuses on gathering civil information to enhance situational understanding and facilitate decision making. CAO and CMO planners (J-9) and supporting CAPTs, in coordination with the CMOC, integrate CR results into the overall OPLAN. Potential sources of civil information that a coordinated CR plan considers include the following:

1. Ongoing assessments of the JOA that identify MOE trends.

2. Identified unknowns in civil information.

3. Gaps identified during collation and analysis.

4. Gaps remaining in the area study, assessment, and staff estimate.

5. CA interaction with IPI or civilian constructs of an operational area, including but not limited to the following:

a. HN government officials.

b. Religious leaders.

c. Tribal, commercial, and private organizations.

d. All categories of DCs.

e. Legal and illegal immigrants.

f. Infrastructure managers and workers.

g. Local industry personnel.

h. Medical and educational personnel.

(d) Data mining is the process of extracting patterns from raw data using sophisticated data search capabilities and statistical algorithms to discover patterns and correlations in large preexisting databases. Data mining uses a combination of open and restricted-source databases for routine and continuous study and research. Data mining is focused by the civil information collection requirements and provides corroboration of other collected civil data. Data mining is focused on the following factors:

1. Priority civil information requirements.

2. Requests for information.

3. Running estimates.

4. Gaps remaining in the area study and area assessment.

(3) **Consolidation** consists of collation and processing.

(a) Collation is the ordering of the data into groupings and focuses on data management. The tools and methods for this step are rapidly maturing. A normalized relational civil information database is capable of cataloging vast amounts of data with attached files and photos and rapidly retrieving this data for follow-on processing, analysis, production, and sharing. Within these database structures, civil information is normally collated by date, type, location, organization, activity, and meta-tagged by supported goals and objectives (e.g., program elements, lines of operation, and/or COM MSRPs depending on the specific mission and supported/supporting relationships).

(b) Processing is the physical and cognitive manipulation of the separate pieces of data into information. Processing structures the collated data into a usable form of information in preparation for analysis.

(4) **Analysis.** Analysis is the process by which collected information is evaluated and integrated with existing information to produce intelligence products that best describe the current and predicts the future impact of the threat and/or environment on operations. Analysts and civil information managers mold the civil information into a usable product. The most difficult analysis performed identifies indicators of future events previously obscured in the background data. CIM supervisors direct the analytical efforts to those gaps

in the commanders' awareness and understanding of the civil component of the operating environment. Analysis of civil information focuses on the following:

1. Identifying mission variables.

2. Identifying operational variables.

3. Identifying COGs.

4. Identifying trends.

5. Conducting predictive analysis.

6. Identifying civil vulnerabilities.

7. Assessment of civil MOPs and MOEs.

8. Prioritization and apportionment of resources to address civil vulnerabilities, influence populations, and legitimize governments.

(5) **Production**

(a) Production is the packaging of civil information products into easily disseminated reports, presentations, and updates. The production phase of the CIM process ensures CIM products and services are relevant, accurate, timely, and useable for commanders and other senior leaders. Following are the products of civil information analysis:

1. Layered geospatial information.

2. Civil layers (ASCOPE) for the COP.

3. COGs.

4. Civil considerations products.

5. Answers to requests for information.

6. Reported priority civil information requirements.

7. Updates to ongoing assessments, estimates, area studies.

(6) **Information Sharing**

(a) Information sharing involves both the active pushing of products to specific consumers through available architectures and the passive posting of products on web portals. The consumers may not realize what they need; therefore, CA/CMO forces must anticipate the information needs of the supported unit or agency. Thorough dissemination of civil information reduces redundancy and ensures that the maximum effects are created by using limited resources to their fullest potential. Mechanisms for dissemination may vary by situation and echelon, but the process and goal remain constant. The J-9 or CMO staff normally serve as the JFC's primary manager for the dissemination and integration of civil information and resultant products. Examples of information sharing include the following:

    1. Integration with the COP.

    2. Establishment of civil information repositories and granting access to online databases that include reports, assessments, and area studies.

    3. Pushing and posting of reports, update briefs, and other civil information products.

    4. Integration with the joint targeting process (nonlethal).

    5. Integration with TCP.

    6. Integration with TCP cycles.

    (b) Civil Information sharing is critical to the efficient pursuit of common goals. Although challenged by cultural and political differences, a collaborative environment facilitates information sharing between many different groups and authorities that can work in parallel. A collaborative environment facilitates information sharing. Although technology can support the creation of an unclassified collaboration and information sharing space, the challenges are largely social, institutional, cultural, and organizational. These impediments can limit and shape the willingness of civilian and military personnel and organizations to openly cooperate and share civil information.

    (c) To overcome barriers to effective communications, the JFC must determine information sharing requirements and provide appropriate disclosure guidance, classifications, and caveats required throughout the civil information lifecycle to enable appropriate mission partners to the maximum extent allowed by US laws and DOD policy. The JFC should recognize the criticality of the civil information sharing function at the outset of complex operations to support unified actions. The JFC should also identify security requirements and vulnerabilities and conduct comprehensive operational risk assessment when sharing civil information.

APPENDIX D
REFERENCES

The development of JP 3-57 is based upon the following primary references.

1. General

a. NSPD-44, *Management of Interagency Efforts Concerning Reconstruction and Stabilization.*

b. *UN CMCoord Officer Field Handbook.*

c. Title 10, USC, *Armed Forces.*

d. Title 22, USC, *Foreign Relations and Intercourse.*

2. Department of Defense Publications

a. *Unified Command Plan.*

b. DOD *Foreign Clearance Guide.*

c. DOD *Foreign Clearance Manual.*

b. DOD 3210.6-R, *Department of Defense Grant and Agreement Regulations.*

c. DODD 1235.10, *Activation, Mobilization, and Demobilization of the Ready Reserve.*

d. DODD 2000.13, *Civil Affairs.*

e. DODD 3000.07, *Irregular Warfare.*

f. DODD 3000.3, *Policy for Nonlethal Weapons.*

g. DODD 5100.46, *Foreign Disaster Relief (FDR).*

h. DODD 5230.11, *Disclosure of Classified Military Information to Foreign Governments and International Organizations.*

i. DODI 2205.02, *Humanitarian and Civic Assistance (HCA) Activities.*

j. DODI 3000.05, *Stability Operations.*

k. DODM 5200.01, Volumes 1-4, *DOD Information Security Program.*

3. Chairman of the Joint Chiefs of Staff Publications

a. CJCSI 3207.01B, *Military Support to Humanitarian Mine Actions.*

b. CJCSI 3214.01B, *Military Support to Foreign Consequence Management Operations*.

c. CJCSI 3214.01D, *Defense Support for Chemical, Biological, Radiological, and Nuclear Incidents on Foreign Territory*.

d. CJCSM 3130.03, *Adaptive Planning and Execution (APEX) Planning Formats and Guidance*.

e. JP 1, *Doctrine for the Armed Forces of the United States*.

f. JP 1-04, *Legal Support to Military Operations*.

g. JP 1-05, *Religious Affairs in Joint Operations*.

h. JP 1-06, *Financial Management Support in Joint Operations*.

i. JP 2-01, *Joint and National Intelligence Support to Military Operations*.

j. JP 2-01.3, *Joint Intelligence Preparation of the Operational Environment*.

k. JP 3-0, *Joint Operations*.

l. JP 3-05, *Special Operations*.

m. JP 3-06, *Joint Urban Operations*.

n. JP 3-07. *Stability Operations*.

o. JP 3-07.2, *Antiterrorism*.

p. JP 3-07.3, *Peace Operations*.

q. JP 3-08, *Interorganizational Coordination During Joint Operations*.

r. JP 3-10, *Joint Security Operations in Theater*.

s. JP 3-11, *Operations in Chemical, Biological, Radiological, and Nuclear (CBRN) Environments*.

t. JP 3-13, *Information Operations*.

u. JP 3-13.2, *Military Information Support Operations*.

v. JP 3-13.3, *Operations Security*.

w. JP 3-15, *Barriers, Obstacles, and Mine Warfare for Joint Operations*.

x. JP 3-16, *Multinational Operations*.

y. JP 3-22, *Foreign Internal Defense.*

z. JP 3-24, *Counterinsurgency Operations.*

aa. JP 3-29, *Foreign Humanitarian Assistance.*

bb. JP 3-33, *Joint Task Force Headquarters.*

cc. JP 3-34, *Joint Engineer Operations.*

dd. JP 3-35, *Deployment and Redeployment Operations.*

ee. JP 3-40, *Countering Weapons of Mass Destruction.*

ff. JP 3-41, *Chemical, Biological, Radiological, and Nuclear Consequence Management.*

gg. JP 3-61, *Public Affairs.*

hh. JP 3-68, *Noncombatant Evacuation Operations.*

ii. JP 4-0, *Joint Logistics.*

jj. JP 4-01, *The Defense Transportation System.*

kk. JP 4-02, *Health Services.*

ll. JP 4-05, *Joint Mobilization Planning.*

mm. JP 4-06, *Mortuary Affairs.*

nn. JP 4-10, *Operational Contract Support.*

oo. JP 5-0, *Joint Operation Planning.*

pp. JP 6-0, *Joint Communications System.*

qq. JP 6-01, *Joint Electromagnetic Spectrum Management Operations.*

4. **Allied Joint Publication**

AJP 3.4.9, *Allied Joint Doctrine for Civil-Military Cooperation.*

5. **United States Army Publications**

a. Army Regulation 195-2, *Criminal Investigation Activities.*

b. FM 3-24, *Counterinsurgency.*

c. FM 3-34, *Engineer Operations.*

d. FM 3-39, *Military Police Operations.*

e. FM 3-57, *Civil Affairs Operations.*

6. **United States Marine Corps Publications**

a. MCWP 3-33.1, *Marine Air-Ground Task Force Civil-Military Operations.*

b. MCWP 3-33.5, *Counterinsurgency.*

c. MCWP 4-11.5/4-04.1M, *Seabee Operations in the MAGTF.*

7. **United States Navy Publications**

a. NTTP 3-02.14 (Rev A), *The Naval Beach Group.*

b. NTTP 4-02.4, *Expeditionary Medical Facilities.*

c. NTTP 4-04.1, *Seabee Operations in the MAGTF.*

d. NTTP 4-04.6, *Hospital Ships.*

e. Navy Technical Reference Publication 4-04.2.1, *Doctrinal Reference for the Naval Construction Force.*

f. NWP 3-02.1, *Ship to Shore Movement.*

g. NWP 3-29, *Disaster Response Operations.*

h. NWP 4-04, *Navy Civil Engineering Operations.*

8. **United States Special Operations Command Publications**

a. USSOCOM Publication 1, *Doctrine for Special Operations.*

b. USSOCOM Directive 525-38, *Civil Military Engagement.*

c. *Joint Civil Information Management Tactical Handbook.*

9. **Multi-Service Publications**

Marine Corps warfighting publication (MCWP) 4-11.5/Navy Tactics, Techniques, and Procedures (NTTP) 4-04.1M, *Seabee Operations in the MAGTF.*

APPENDIX E
ADMINISTRATIVE INSTRUCTIONS

1. User Comments

Users in the field are highly encouraged to submit comments on this publication to: Joint Staff J-7, Deputy Director, Joint Education and Doctrine, ATTN: Joint Doctrine Analysis Division, 116 Lake View Parkway, Suffolk, VA 23435-2697. These comments should address content (accuracy, usefulness, consistency, and organization), writing, and appearance.

2. Authorship

The lead agent for this publication is the United States Special Operations Command. The Joint Staff doctrine sponsor for this publication is the Director for Operations (J-3).

3. Supersession

This publication supersedes JP 3-57, 8 July 2008, *Civil-Military Operations*.

4. Change Recommendations

a. Recommendations for urgent changes to this publication should be submitted:

   TO: JOINT STAFF WASHINGTON DC//J7-JE&D//

b. Routine changes should be submitted electronically to the Deputy Director, Joint Education and Doctrine, ATTN: Joint Doctrine Analysis Division, 116 Lake View Parkway, Suffolk, VA 23435 2697, and info the lead agent and the Director for Joint Force Development, J-7/JE&D.

c. When a Joint Staff directorate submits a proposal to the CJCS that would change source document information reflected in this publication, that directorate will include a proposed change to this publication as an enclosure to its proposal. The Services and other organizations are requested to notify the Joint Staff J-7 when changes to source documents reflected in this publication are initiated.

5. Distribution of Publications

Local reproduction is authorized, and access to unclassified publications is unrestricted. However, access to and reproduction authorization for classified JPs must be IAW DOD Manual 5200.01, Volume 1, *DOD Information Security Program: Overview, Classification, and Declassification,* and DOD Manual 5200.01, Volume 3, *DOD Information Security Program: Protection of Classified Information.*

6. Distribution of Electronic Publications

a. Joint Staff J-7 will not print copies of JPs for distribution. Electronic versions are available on JDEIS at https://jdeis.js.mil (NIPRNET) and http://jdeis.js.smil.mil (SIPRNET), and on the JEL at http://www.dtic.mil/doctrine (NIPRNET).

b. Only approved JPs and joint test publications are releasable outside the CCMDs, Services, and Joint Staff. Release of any classified JP to foreign governments or foreign nationals must be requested through the local embassy (Defense Attaché Office) to DIA, Defense Foreign Liaison/IE-3, 200 MacDill Blvd., Joint Base Anacostia-Bolling, Washington, DC 20340-5100.

c. JEL CD-ROM. Upon request of a joint doctrine development community member, the Joint Staff J-7 will produce and deliver one CD-ROM with current JPs. This JEL CD-ROM will be updated not less than semi-annually and when received can be locally reproduced for use within the CCMDs, Services, and combat support agencies.

GLOSSARY
PART I—ABBREVIATIONS AND ACRONYMS

AC	Active Component
ADR	airfield damage repair
AFCAP	Air Force contract augmentation program
AFMS	Air Force Medical Service
AFOSI	Air Force Office of Special Investigations
AJP	allied joint publication
ANG	Air National Guard
AOR	area of responsibility
APEX	Adaptive Planning and Execution
ASCC	Army Service component command
ASCOPE	areas, structures, capabilities, organizations, people, and events
AT	antiterrorism
BCT	brigade combat teams
BIA	behavioral influences analysis
C2	command and control
CA	civil affairs
CACOM	civil affairs command
CAG	civil affairs group
CAO	civil affairs operations
CAPT	civil affairs planning team
CAT	civil affairs team
CBMU	construction battalion maintenance unit
CBRN	chemical, biological, radiological, and nuclear
CCDR	combatant commander
CCIR	commander's critical information requirement
CCMD	combatant command
CDRUSSOCOM	Commander, United States Special Operations Command
CDRUSTRANSCOM	Commander, United States Transportation Command
CEB	combat engineer battalion
CF	conventional forces
CIM	civil information management
CIMIC	civil-military cooperation
CJCS	Chairman of the Joint Chiefs of Staff
CJCSI	Chairman of the Joint Chiefs of Staff instruction
CJCSM	Chairman of the Joint Chiefs of Staff manual
CLT	civil liaison team
CME	civil-military engagement
CMO	civil-military operations
CMOC	civil-military operations center
CMSE	civil-military support element
COA	course of action

COCOM	combatant command (command authority)
COG	center of gravity
COIN	counterinsurgency
COM	chief of mission
CONUS	continental United States
COP	common operational picture
COS	chief of staff
CR	civil reconnaissance
CRC	crisis reaction center
DC	dislocated civilian
DOD	Department of Defense
DODD	Department of Defense directive
DODI	Department of Defense instruction
DODM	Department of Defense manual
DOS	Department of State
EMD	expeditionary military information support detachment
EMT	expeditionary military information support team
EOD	explosive ordnance disposal
ESB	engineer support battalion
FCM	foreign consequence management
FHA	foreign humanitarian assistance
FHP	force health protection
FID	foreign internal defense
FM	field manual (Army)
FN	foreign nation
FNS	foreign nation support
FORSCOM	United States Army Forces Command
FP	force protection
FPA	foreign policy advisor
GCC	geographic combatant commander
GE	general engineering
HA	humanitarian assistance
HACC	humanitarian assistance coordination center
HCA	humanitarian and civic assistance
HD	harbor defense
HHC	headquarters and headquarters company
HN	host nation
HNS	host-nation support
HOC	humanitarian operations center
IGO	intergovernmental organization

IHS	international health specialist
IM	information management
IO	information operations
IPI	indigenous populations and institutions
IRC	information-related capability
IW	irregular warfare
J-2	intelligence directorate of a joint staff
J-3	operations directorate of a joint staff
J-9	civil-military operations directorate of a joint staff
JCMOTF	joint civil-military operations task force
JFC	joint force commander
JFCH	joint force chaplain
JFMCC	joint force maritime component commander
JIACG	joint interagency coordination group
JIPOE	joint intelligence preparation of the operational environment
JLLIS	Joint Lessons Learned Information System
JMISTF	joint military information support task force
JOA	joint operations area
JOPP	joint operation planning process
JP	joint publication
JPASE	Joint Public Affairs Support Element
JSOTF	joint special operations task force
JTF	joint task force
LE	law enforcement
LOE	line of effort
LOO	line of operation
MAGTF	Marine air-ground task force
MCA	military civic action
MCAST	maritime civil affairs and security training
MCAT	maritime civil affairs team
MCMO	medical civil-military operations
MCWP	Marine Corps warfighting publication
MEF	Marine expeditionary force
MESF	maritime expeditionary security force
MIS	military information support
MISG	military information support group
MISO	military information support operations
MISTF	military information support task force
MLG	Marine logistics group
MNF	multinational force
MOE	measure of effectiveness
MOP	measure of performance
MP	military police (Army and Marine)

MSRP	mission strategic resource plan
MWSS	Marine wing support squadron
NA	nation assistance
NATO	North Atlantic Treaty Organization
NAVFAC	Naval Facilities Engineering Command
NBG	naval beach group
NCC	Navy component commander
NCF	naval construction force
NCR	naval construction regiment
NECC	Navy Expeditionary Combat Command
NEO	noncombatant evacuation operation
NGO	nongovernmental organization
NMCB	naval mobile construction battalion
NSC	National Security Council
NSPD	national security Presidential directive
NTTP	Navy tactics, techniques, and procedures
NWP	Navy warfare publication
O&I	operations and intelligence
OCONUS	outside the continental United States
OE	operational environment
OFDA	Office of United States Foreign Disaster Assistance (USAID)
OIC	officer in charge
OPSEC	operations security
OSD	Office of the Secretary of Defense
PA	public affairs
PAO	public affairs officer
PHIBCB	amphibious construction battalion
PIR	priority intelligence requirement
PO	peace operations
PRC	populace and resources control
Prime BEEF	Prime Base Engineer Emergency Force
PRT	provincial reconstruction team
PS	port security
RC	Reserve Component
RED HORSE	Rapid Engineer Deployable Heavy Operational Repair Squadron Engineer
RM	resource management
ROE	rules of engagement
SCA	support to civil administration
SecDef	Secretary of Defense
SJA	staff judge advocate

SOF	special operations forces
SSR	security sector reform
SYG	Secretary-General (UN)
TCP	theater campaign plan
TEC	theater engineer command
TIM	toxic industrial material
TSOC	theater special operations command
UCT	underwater construction team
UN	United Nations
UN CMCoord	United Nations humanitarian civil-military coordination
UNDPKO	United Nations Department for Peacekeeping Operations
UNHCHR	United Nations High Commissioner for Human Rights
UNOCHA	United Nations Office for the Coordination of Humanitarian Affairs
USA	United States Army
USACE	United States Army Corps of Engineers
USACIDC	United States Army Criminal Investigation Command
USAF	United States Air Force
USAID	United States Agency for International Development
USAR	United States Army Reserve
USASOC	United States Army Special Operations Command
USC	United States Code
USCG	United States Coast Guard
USDAO	United States defense attaché office
USD(P)	Under Secretary of Defense for Policy
USG	United States Government
USMC	United States Marine Corps
USN	United States Navy
USSOCOM	United States Special Operations Command
WHO	World Health Organization (UN)
WMD	weapons of mass destruction

PART II—TERMS AND DEFINITIONS

civic action. None. (Approved for removal from JP 1-02.)

civil affairs. Designated Active and Reserve Component forces and units organized, trained, and equipped specifically to conduct civil affairs operations and to support civil-military operations. Also called **CA.** (JP 1-02. SOURCE: JP 3-57)

civil affairs operations. Actions planned, executed, and assessed by civil affairs forces that enhance awareness of and manage the interaction with the civil component of the operational environment; identify and mitigate underlying causes of instability within civil society; or involve the application of functional specialty skills normally the responsibility of civil government. Also called **CAO.** (Approved for incorporation into JP 1-02.)

civil information. Relevant data relating to the civil areas, structures, capabilities, organizations, people, and events of the civil component of the operational environment used to support the situational awareness of the supported commander. (Approved for inclusion in JP 1-02.)

civil information management. Process whereby data relating to the civil component of the operational environment is gathered, collated, processed, analyzed, produced into information products, and disseminated. Also called **CIM.** (Approved for inclusion in JP 1-02.)

civil-military operations. Activities of a commander performed by designated civil affairs or other military forces that establish, maintain, influence, or exploit relations between military forces, indigenous populations, and institutions, by directly supporting the attainment of objectives relating to the reestablishment or maintenance of stability within a region or host nation. Also called **CMO.** (Approved for incorporation into JP 1-02.)

civil-military operations center. An organization, normally comprised of civil affairs, established to plan and facilitate coordination of activities of the Armed Forces of the United States within indigenous populations and institutions, the private sector, intergovernmental organizations, nongovernmental organizations, multinational forces, and other governmental agencies in support of the joint force commander. Also called **CMOC.** (Approved for incorporation into JP 1-02.)

civil-military team. A temporary organization of civilian and military personnel task-organized to provide an optimal mix of capabilities and expertise to accomplish specific operational and planning tasks. (Approved for inclusion in JP 1-02.)

civil reconnaissance. A targeted, planned, and coordinated observation and evaluation of specific civil aspects of the environment such as areas, structures, capabilities, organizations, people, or events. Also called **CR.** (Approved for inclusion in JP 1-02.)

evacuee. A civilian removed from a place of residence by military direction for reasons of personal security or the requirements of the military situation. (JP 1-02. SOURCE: JP 3-57)

expellee. None. (Approved for removal from JP 1-02.)

host nation. A nation which receives the forces and/or supplies of allied nations and/or NATO organizations to be located on, to operate in, or to transit through its territory. Also called **HN.** (JP 1-02. SOURCE: JP 3-57)

humanitarian assistance. None. (Approved for removal from JP 1-02.)

indigenous populations and institutions. The societal framework of an operational environment including citizens, legal and illegal immigrants, dislocated civilians, and governmental, tribal, ethnic, religious, commercial, and private organizations and entities. Also called **IPI.** (Approved for incorporation into JP 1-02.)

joint civil-military operations task force. A joint task force composed of civil-military operations units from more than one Service. Also called **JCMOTF.** (Approved for incorporation into JP 1-02.)

military civic action. Programs and projects managed by United States forces but executed primarily by indigenous military or security forces that contribute to the economic and social development of a host nation civil society thereby enhancing the legitimacy and social standing of the host nation government and its military forces. Also called **MCA.** (Approved for incorporation into JP 1-02.)

military government. The supreme authority the military exercises by force or agreement over the lands, property, and indigenous populations and institutions of domestic, allied, or enemy territory therefore substituting sovereign authority under rule of law for the previously established government. (Approved for incorporation into JP 1-02.)

private sector. An umbrella term that may be applied to any or all of the nonpublic or commercial individuals and businesses, specified nonprofit organizations, most of academia and other scholastic institutions, and selected nongovernmental organizations. (Approved for incorporation into JP 1-02.)

provincial reconstruction team. A civil-military team designated to improve stability in a given area by helping build the legitimacy and effectiveness of a host nation local or provincial government in providing security to its citizens and delivering essential government services. Also called **PRT.** (Approved for incorporation into JP 1-02.)

Intentionally Blank

JOINT DOCTRINE PUBLICATIONS HIERARCHY

JP 1
JOINT DOCTRINE
JP 1-0
PERSONNEL
JP 2-0
INTELLIGENCE
JP 3-0
OPERATIONS
JP 4-0
LOGISTICS
JP 5-0
PLANS
JP 6-0
COMMUNICATIONS SYSTEM

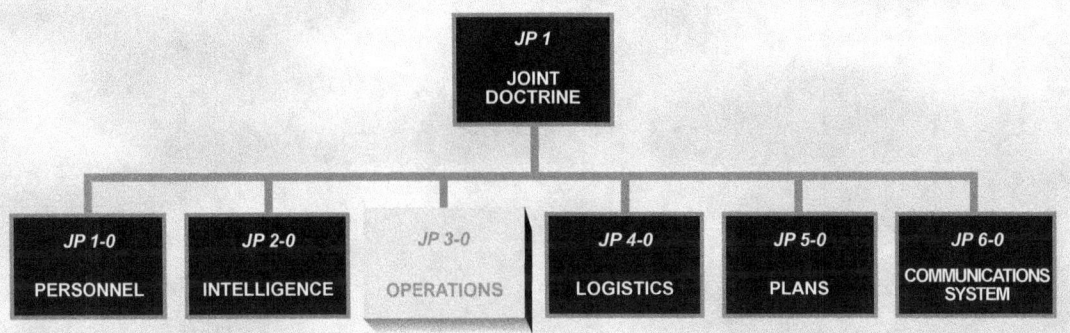

All joint publications are organized into a comprehensive hierarchy as shown in the chart above. **Joint Publication (JP) 3-57** is in the **Operations** series of joint doctrine publications. The diagram below illustrates an overview of the development process:

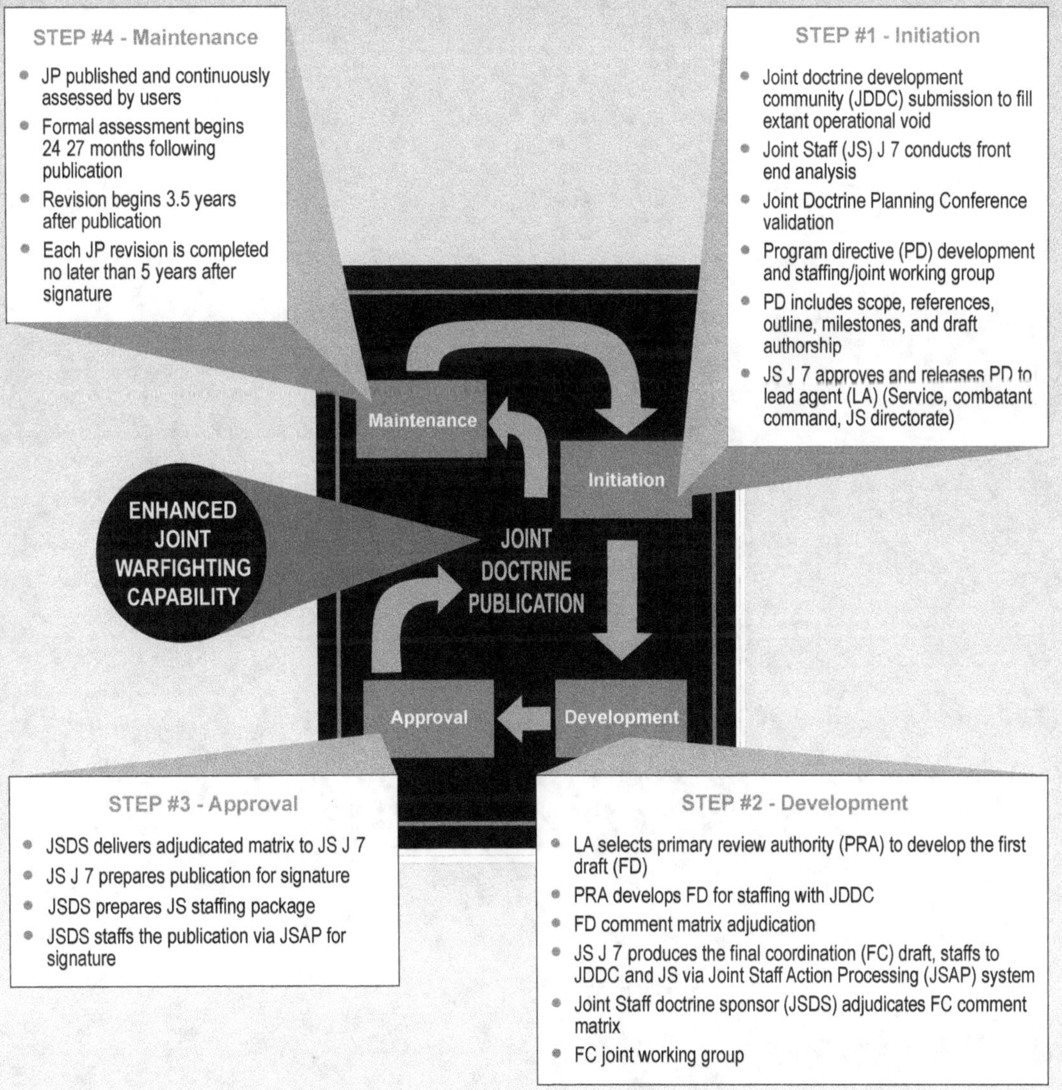

STEP #4 - Maintenance
JP published and continuously assessed by users
Formal assessment begins 24 27 months following publication
Revision begins 3.5 years after publication
Each JP revision is completed no later than 5 years after signature
STEP #1 - Initiation
Joint doctrine development community (JDDC) submission to fill extant operational void
Joint Staff (JS) J 7 conducts front end analysis
Joint Doctrine Planning Conference validation
Program directive (PD) development and staffing/joint working group
PD includes scope, references, outline, milestones, and draft authorship
JS J 7 approves and releases PD to lead agent (LA) (Service, combatant command, JS directorate)
Maintenance
Initiation
ENHANCED JOINT WARFIGHTING CAPABILITY
JOINT DOCTRINE PUBLICATION
Approval
Development
STEP #3 - Approval
JSDS delivers adjudicated matrix to JS J 7
JS J 7 prepares publication for signature
JSDS prepares JS staffing package
JSDS staffs the publication via JSAP for signature
STEP #2 - Development
LA selects primary review authority (PRA) to develop the first draft (FD)
PRA develops FD for staffing with JDDC
FD comment matrix adjudication
JS J 7 produces the final coordination (FC) draft, staffs to JDDC and JS via Joint Staff Action Processing (JSAP) system
Joint Staff doctrine sponsor (JSDS) adjudicates FC comment matrix
FC joint working group

www.ingramcontent.com/pod-product-compliance
Lightning Source LLC
Chambersburg PA
CBHW081325310526
45789CB00018B/2361